THE
Southern
Entertainer's
Cookbook

THE
Southern
Entertainer's
Cookbook

Heirloom Recipes *for* Modern Gatherings

Courtney Whitmore

Photographs by Kyle Dreier

GIBBS SMITH
TO ENRICH AND INSPIRE HUMANKIND

First Edition

24 23 22 21 20   1 2 3 4 5

Text © 2020 Courtney Whitmore
Photographs © 2020 Kyle Dreier / Dreier & Company LLC

Published by
Gibbs Smith
P.O. Box 667
Layton, Utah 84041

1.800.835.4993 orders
www.gibbs-smith.com

Designed by Jan Derevjanik
Printed and bound in China

Gibbs Smith books are printed on either recycled, 100%
post-consumer waste, FSC-certified papers or on paper
produced from sustainable PEFC-certified forest/controlled
wood source. Learn more at www.pefc.org.

Library of Congress Cataloging-in-Publication Data

Names: Whitmore, Courtney Dial, author. |
Dreier, Kyle, photographer.
Title: The southern entertainer's cookbook : heirloom
recipes for modern gatherings / Courtney Whitmore;
photographs by Kyle Dreier.
Description: First edition. | Layton : Gibbs Smith, [2020] |
Includes index. | Summary: "Serve up classic recipes and
new favorites from a Southern perspective. Courtney is
known for creating delicious, party-friendly food to enhance
any meal and every party"— Provided by publisher.
Identifiers: LCCN 2019054772 | ISBN 9781423653103
(hardcover) | ISBN 9781423653110 (epub)
Subjects: LCSH: Cooking, American—Southern style. |
LCGFT: Cookbooks.
Classification: LCC TX715.2.S68 W477 2020 |
DDC 641.5975—dc23
LC record available at https://lccn.loc.gov/2019054772

For Jayne and Jessica,
our two best friends.

Contents

Introduction

I am proud to be from the South—where tea is sweet and accents are sweeter;
summer starts in April; front porches are wide and words are long;
macaroni and cheese is a vegetable; pecan pie is a staple;
y'all is the only proper pronoun; chicken is fried and biscuits come with gravy;
everything is darling and someone is always getting their heart blessed.
Have a good day y'all!
—SOUTHERN SAYING

Entertaining is a way of life in the South; it's as ingrained in our culture as sweet tea and one hundred percent humidity. We have no shortage of reasons to invite friends and family over and we always have room for one more. Born and raised here in the South, I'm proud of our rich heritage of Southern hospitality. No matter whether we're polishing the silver and pulling out the fine china for a high falutin' to-do or eating hand pies on the back porch, food is at the heart of all celebrations.

Growing up, I always loved hearing my mom say "company's coming." I have fond childhood memories of peeking through the stair rails from the second floor of our downtown Charleston home as my mother graciously greeted cocktail party guests and led them into the formal dining room for drinks and hors d'oeuvres. My brother and I would wait until everyone was busy laughing the night away and then dart downstairs to sneak two pieces of chocolate fudge off the silver platter, and hope we wouldn't get caught. Of course, we knew exactly where they would be located because our mother labeled all her dishes and silver trays with sticky notes in the days leading up to the party. She was the quintessential Southern hostess, having learned the art of entertaining from her parents at a very young age.

From hosting elegant tea parties in her garden to formal Christmas cocktail parties, these festivities instilled in me a passion for entertaining and Southern food. My mother organized all her best Southern recipes in a large binder, which sat on our kitchen counter, and she would flip through it to create her party menus for every special occasion. My hope is that this book becomes your own go-to collection of recipes for a lifetime of celebrations.

In our family, we regard our recipes with as much importance as our family photo albums. They've been handed down through generations, bringing special pleasures and providing unforgettable memories to every family member. My grandfather was one of the best scratch cooks I've known. You'll also find many of his beloved favorites within these pages.

Both my grandmothers made Southern entertaining look like a breeze. They whipped up prize-winning pies, vacuumed every nook and cranny of their home, and welcomed dinner party guests by evening, all while wearing heels and pearls. They made it all look so effortless when in actuality, as every hostess knows, there is quite a bit of work that happens up front. While entertaining is much more casual and impromptu these days, I hope this book helps simplify the process. Parties don't have to be formal and fussy; the next time you and your friends want to get together, try a little front porch sitt'n and sweet tea sippin'. The only "rule" you need to follow is to never run out of food—but if you do, pull out an extra can of seasoned pecans and keep the party rollin'. You might just find entertaining becomes your very favorite pastime!

One last thing! The best pieces of advice about cooking that my grandmother taught me is to read through the entire recipe before starting and taste along the way.

> *"A shared recipe in the South is more precious than gold*
> *. . . and it always comes with a story."*
> —SOUTHERN SAYING

We hope these shared recipes bring you as much joy at your parties and celebrations as they have brought us over the years.

Courtney & Co.

Party Portions
&
Planning

We all know that the secret to any party is a great guest list and delicious food. Start with the number of guests when planning out any celebration, big or small. You'll want to determine how many mouths to feed, after all. Next, decide if you're throwing a party with heavy hors d'oeuvres and appetizers or entrées at a seated luncheon or dinner party.

Appetizers are the star of the show at occasions like cocktail parties, bridal showers, and holiday parties. If guests are standing, be sure to select easy "pick-up foods" that don't require cutlery. Aim for a larger number of savory selections than desserts, but always include a few sweet bites as well. Serve a variety of flavors and types of appetizers (hot and cold, spicy and mild, meat and vegetarian, etc). There is no official rule, but I aim to serve five to seven types of appetizers and two to three types of mini desserts at any gathering of more than ten people.

For entrée occasions, begin with one or two bite-size appetizers, a main dish, and a spattering of sides and salads. Finish with a signature layer cake or two or three smaller dessert options, like pies. Don't forget cocktails and always include sweet tea!

The recipes in this book are meant to help guide your menu preparations. Many themed parties and occasions are listed on the following two pages as a starting place for your party menu. Mix and match them for your own special celebrations and occasions.

Party Menus

FOOTBALL TAILGATE & GAME DAY PARTY

Nashville Hot Chicken Biscuits
(page 18)

Game Day Chili Bread Bowls
(page 78)

Black Bean Salad (page 57)

Baked Cheesy Corn Dip
(page 35)

Chocolate Chunk Pecan Cookies
(page 114)

BABY SHOWER OR BRIDAL SHOWER

Hot Chicken Salad (page 72)

Mini BLT Salads (page 51)

Crispy Pimento Cheese Cups
(page 31)

Southern Almond Tea Cakes
(page 128)

Sour Cream Pound Cake (page 140) with Fruit

Perfect Party Punch (page 201)

Mini Classic Southern Biscuits
(page 98)

Mini Phronsie's Banana Muffins (page 108)

PICNIC PARTY

Southern Charcuterie Board
(page 45)

Jalapeño & Bacon Deviled Eggs
(page 21)

Butter Bean Salad (page 56)

Strawberry Pie (page 172)

Lemon Squares (page 147)

SIPS & SWEETS BIRTHDAY CELEBRATION

Sparkling Apple Cider Sangria
(page 185)

Orange Mimosa Floats
(page 190)

Perfect Party Punch (page 201)

Caramel Celebration Cake
(page 136)

Brown Sugar Pie (page 164)

Key Lime Trifles (page 150)

Peach Lattice Cobbler
(page 167)

PORCH PARTY

Tea Party Sandwiches
(page 28)

Petite Heirloom Tomato Pies
(page 25)

Summer Melon Ball Salad
(page 59)

Strawberry Cake (page 144)

Cream Cheese Cookies
(page 117)

Grapefruit Shoo-Fly Punch
(page 194)

EASTER BRUNCH

Orange-Glazed Ham (page 77)

Ham Hock Green Beans
(page 85)

Southern Spoon Bread
(page 102)

Squash Casserole (page 92)

Jalapeño & Bacon Deviled Eggs
(page 21)

Old-Fashioned Coconut Cake
(page 139)

Southern Sweet Tea (page 186)

CHRISTMAS COCKTAIL & DESSERT PARTY

BACKYARD BBQ

SOUTHERN DINNER PARTY

SUNDAY SUPPER

BREAKFAST BRUNCH PARTY

NEW YEAR'S EVE PARTY

Appetizers & Party Bites

Delight your guests with these little pick-me-ups of Southern goodness.

Nashville Hot Chicken Biscuits

Yield: 24 hot chicken biscuits

Peanut oil for frying

$^1/_2$ cup buttermilk

2 eggs

1 tablespoon hot sauce

1 cup all-purpose flour

1 tablespoon salt

1 tablespoon black pepper

1 pound boneless, skinless chicken breasts or chicken thighs

2 tablespoons cayenne pepper

$^1/_2$ teaspoon garlic powder

1 teaspoon paprika

1 teaspoon brown sugar

$^1/_2$ cup butter, melted

24 prepared mini biscuits; use 1$^1/_2$-inch cutters for biscuit dough to create mini biscuits (see recipe on page 98)

8 baby gherkin pickles, sliced

Prince's Hot Chicken Shack made Nashville famous for this spicy specialty. Nowadays, you'll find hot chicken on menus throughout Music City and all over the country. There's even an annual Nashville Hot Chicken Festival. We've turned this spicy favorite into a bite-size Southern appetizer that's perfect for parties and tailgates. You can also switch out yeast rolls or mini waffles for the biscuits.

In a Dutch oven or wide, deep pan, heat 2–3 inches of peanut oil to 350 degrees F. In a shallow bowl, whisk together buttermilk with eggs and hot sauce. In a second shallow bowl, combine flour, salt, and black pepper. Cut chicken into 1$^1/_2$-inch pieces. Coat each chicken piece in flour mixture, dip into egg mixture, and then back again in flour mixture. Fry chicken in batches (2–3 minutes on each side), being careful not to overcrowd the pan, until lightly golden (internal temperature measuring 165 degrees F). Place fried chicken pieces onto a rack to cool.

In a small mixing bowl, combine cayenne pepper, garlic powder, paprika, brown sugar, and melted butter. Brush mixture onto each fried chicken piece. Place fried chicken pieces inside biscuits and top with a pickle slice.

TIP: *If you're not a fan of spice, simply leave out the hot sauce and cayenne pepper. Mini biscuits are great for filling with sliced ham or turkey as well.*

Jalapeño & Bacon Deviled Eggs

Yield: 12 deviled eggs

6 eggs, hard-boiled and peeled

¼ cup mayonnaise

2 teaspoons yellow mustard

⅛ teaspoon cayenne pepper

½ teaspoon salt

½ teaspoon Worcestershire sauce

1 tablespoon sweet pickle relish

4 slices cooked bacon, chopped

1 jalapeño, seeded and sliced

Chives and paprika, for garnish

You won't attend a picnic down South without finding at least one variety of this classic appetizer. Deviled eggs are one of the first party bites to disappear right off the platter. Kick the typical deviled eggs up a notch with this jalapeño and bacon version.

Cut eggs in half and remove the yolks. Add yolks to mixing bowl and mash together with mayonnaise, mustard, red pepper, salt, Worcestershire sauce, and pickle relish until well combined. Add additional mayonnaise if needed.

Be sure each egg half rests nicely on your serving platter. If necessary, carefully slice a bit off the bottom so it rests evenly. Spoon yolk mixture into the egg halves. Top with bacon, a jalapeño slice, chives, and a dash of paprika.

Lowcountry Shrimp 'n' Grits

Yield: 8 servings

CHEESE GRITS

2 cups chicken broth

2 cups 2 percent milk

¾ cup butter, cubed

1 teaspoon salt

1 teaspoon pepper

1 cup uncooked old-fashioned grits

1 cup grated sharp cheddar cheese

Native to lowcountry South Carolina, shrimp 'n' grits is arguably one of the most iconic Southern dishes. Creamy cheese grits are given an upscale twist when topped with sautéed shrimp for what we consider to be the quintessential Southern appetizer. Serve these mini shrimp 'n' grits in stemware on your grandmother's silver platter.

CHEESE GRITS

In a large saucepan, bring broth, milk, butter, salt, and pepper to a boil. Slowly stir in grits and reduce heat to medium low. Cover and allow to cook for 12–13 minutes (or until thickened). Be sure to stir occasionally. Stir in cheese and keep warm. Top with additional cheese, if desired.

BOILED SHRIMP

2 tablespoons olive oil

1 pound uncooked medium shrimp, peeled and deveined

1 teaspoon Old Bay Seasoning

½ teaspoon cayenne pepper

3 cloves garlic, minced

1 teaspoon finely diced chives

Paprika, for garnish

BOILED SHRIMP

Heat olive oil in a skillet over medium heat. Add shrimp and sprinkle with Old Bay Seasoning and cayenne pepper. Stir in garlic. Saute shrimp until pink and opaque, 2–3 minutes. The most important thing to know about cooking shrimp is when to stop. They cook quickly, so watch carefully to avoid overcooking.

Fill each appetizer cup with Cheese Grits and top with 3 or 4 shrimp. Garnish each with chives and a sprinkle of paprika. You can also add extra cheddar cheese.

TIP: *Short stemmed glassware, such as sherry or brandy glasses, are a must-have for any hostess. They can be filled with savory appetizers—like shrimp 'n' grits or dips with veggies—as well as sweet treats like ice cream or mini yogurt parfaits for brunch.*

Petite Heirloom Tomato Pies

Yield: 30 petite pies

2 unbaked pie crusts

2 cups mini heirloom tomatoes

1 teaspoon salt

2 tablespoons mayonnaise

1 cup grated pepper jack cheese

¼ teaspoon ground black pepper

Basil and chives, for garnish

These flaky heirloom tomato pies are the perfect summer appetizer for showers, reunions, and parties. I didn't inherit my mother's green thumb, but basil and chives are two foolproof herbs to grow. I cut them fresh from a pot on my back porch for garnishing these mini pies.

Preheat oven to 450 degrees F.

Roll out pie crusts and cut into circles using a 2-inch round cookie cutter or fluted round ravioli cutter. Press pie crusts gently into a mini muffin tin sprayed with nonstick cooking spray. Keep tin refrigerated until ready to fill.

Slice the tomatoes very thin and place on a paper towel. Salt lightly, flip each tomato slice over, and salt again. In a small mixing bowl, stir together mayonnaise, cheese, and pepper.

Scoop 1 teaspoon of mixture into each pie crust. Top each with several slices of tomatoes. Bake for 8–10 minutes or until lightly golden. Garnish with basil and chives.

Poppie's Fig Jam & Prosciutto Crostini

Yield: 24 crostini

POPPIE'S FIG JAM

2 cups figs, stems removed and sliced in half

2 cups sugar

1 lemon, thinly sliced and seeds removed

¼ cup Grand Marnier

I have fond memories of picking figs off my grandparent's fig tree in Belton, South Carolina. My grandfather "Poppie" could make this fig jam in his sleep, and we always left their house with jars and jars of fig jam every summer. Poppie taught my mother and she taught me. Fig jam is absolutely divine spread on toast, waffles, baked brie, or crostini.

POPPIE'S FIG JAM

Wash figs in cold water and drain. Place figs in a large saucepan and cover with sugar. Allow figs to sit overnight.

The next day, add lemon slices to the fig pan and bring to a boil over medium-high heat. Stir often. After mixture begins to boil, reduce heat to low and simmer for 1 hour, stirring often. Remove from stove and allow to cool to room temperature. Add fig mixture to blender and blend until pureed. Stir in Grand Marnier and pour fig jam into sterilized jars with tops. Keep refrigerated.

ASSEMBLING THE CROSTINI

24 slices baguette (1 to 2 loaves)

2 tablespoons olive oil

2 teaspoons sea salt

8 ounces soft goat cheese (chèvre)

8 ounces Poppie's Fig Jam

12 slices prosciutto

ASSEMBLING THE CROSTINI

Preheat oven to 350 degrees F.

Place baguette slices on a baking sheet and brush with olive oil. Sprinkle with sea salt. Bake for 10 minutes or until lightly toasted.

Spread each slice with goat cheese. Top each with a generous spread of fig jam. Cut each slice of prosciutto in half and fold one on top of each crostini.

TIP: *Set up a mouthwatering display of cheeses, meats, and jams and let your party guests create their own crostini combinations.*

Tea Party Sandwiches

My mother used to serve these tea sandwiches at her Charleston garden parties. All the ladies would wear fancy hats and nibble their tea sandwiches on the nicest of china. We served these sandwiches at my daughter's fifth birthday, tea party themed, of course. They're perfect for showers, picnics, and porch parties.

Cucumber Tea Sandwiches

Yield: 20 sandwiches

8 ounces cream cheese, softened

¼ cup finely chopped green bell pepper

¼ cup finely chopped scallions

1 cup finely chopped celery

1 tablespoon lemon juice

¼ teaspoon salt

¼ teaspoon pepper

20 slices cucumber (1 to 2 cucumbers)

20 slices thin wheat or white sandwich bread

Fresh dill, for garnish (optional)

Beat the cream cheese with an electric mixer until light and fluffy. Stir in bell pepper, scallions, celery, lemon juice, salt, and pepper. Mix well. Refrigerate until needed.

Cut the bread circles using 2-inch round cookie cutters. One piece of bread should yield 2 circles. Remove the cream cheese mixture from the refrigerator and allow to soften. Spread 40 circles of bread with cream cheese mixture. Top 20 circles with a slice of cucumber, then top with another bread circle. Store in an airtight container in the refrigerator until ready to serve. Garnish with dill just before serving.

TIP: *Tea sandwiches are perfect for serving on cake stands or tiered platters. Tuck in a few floral blooms for a charming touch.*

Rinne's Spinach Tea Sandwiches

Yield: 48 tea sandwiches

1 (10-ounce) package frozen chopped spinach

2 cups mayonnaise

½ cup dried minced onion

½ cup dried parsley

1 tablespoon lemon juice

2 drops hot sauce

1 large loaf wheat or white sandwich bread

Cook the spinach according to package instructions. Drain well to remove all excess moisture, and then pat with paper towels. Combine the spinach with the mayonnaise, onion, parsley, lemon juice, and hot sauce and mix well. Cover and refrigerate the mixture for 2–3 hours, allowing the flavors to blend.

Spread the spinach mixture on half the slices of bread then top with remaining slices. Refrigerate for several hours and then trim crusts from the slices of bread (it makes a cleaner cut when cold). Slice each sandwich into quarters. Store in an airtight container in the refrigerator until ready to serve.

Pimento Cheese Tea Sandwiches

Yield: 24 tea sandwiches

2 cups grated sharp cheddar cheese

1 (4-ounce) jar diced pimentos, undrained

1 cup mayonnaise

⅛ teaspoon salt

¼ teaspoon hot pepper sauce or 1 jalapeño pepper, finely chopped

1 loaf wheat or white sandwich bread

Combine all ingredients until well mixed. Cover and chill for at least 2 hours. Spread pimento cheese evenly across half of bread slices. Top with remaining slices. Refrigerate for several hours and then trim crusts from the slices of bread (it makes a cleaner cut when cold). Cut each sandwich into quarters or bar-size sandwiches. Store in an airtight container in the refrigerator until ready to serve.

Crispy Pimento Cheese Cups

Yield: 36 cups

PIMENTO CHEESE

2 cups grated sharp cheddar cheese

1 (4-ounce) jar diced pimentos, undrained

1 cup high-quality mayonnaise (such as Duke's)

$1/8$ teaspoon salt

$1/4$ teaspoon hot pepper sauce or 1 jalapeño pepper, finely chopped

CRISPY TOAST CUPS

1 loaf thinly sliced sandwich bread

$1/2$ cup butter, softened

Diced chives

Nicknamed "Southern caviar," pimento cheese is a signature spread found throughout Southern cuisine. Whether you're enjoying a pimento cheese sandwich in Augusta, Georgia, at the Masters Tournament or gussying up classic finger foods for a dinner party, pimento cheese is always a favorite. I haven't hosted a party or gathering where these pimento cheese cups weren't on the menu.

PIMENTO CHEESE

Combine all ingredients until well mixed. Cover and chill for at least 2 hours.

TIP: *Chives are a hearty, year-round herb that are easy to grow and perfect for garnishing appetizers.*

CRISPY TOAST CUPS

Preheat oven to 350 degrees F.

Using a rolling pin, roll each slice of bread slightly and use a 2-inch biscuit cutter or cookie cutter to cut out 2 rounds from each slice. Each loaf of bread has about 18 slices, not using the heels. After cutting the bread rounds, brush the inside of a mini muffin pan with butter. Carefully fit the bread rounds into the mini muffin pan. Brush the inside of the bread rounds with butter. Bake the empty cups for 10 minutes. Remove from oven and fill the cups with Pimento Cheese. Bake again for 5–7 minutes. Garnish with diced chives.

These cups are twice baked, making them very crispy and delicious. Toasted cups, before being filled, can also be frozen to be filled and baked at a later time.

TIP: *Crispy toast cups can be used for a variety of hors d'oeuvres. Fill them with anything from chicken salad to spinach artichoke dip for a delicious party bite.*

Marie's Cheese Wafers

Yield: 60 cheese wafers

2 cups grated sharp cheddar cheese

1/2 cup plus 2 tablespoons butter, softened

1 1/2 cups all-purpose flour

1/2 teaspoon salt

1/4 teaspoon cayenne pepper

60 pecan halves (optional)

A twist on the classic cheese straws, my mother acquired this cheese wafer recipe from her college roommate's mother, Marie. She was one of the best cooks in Virginia. Bake these wafers just before friends arrive and your house will smell divine!

In the bowl of a stand mixer, cream cheese and butter together for 2 minutes. Add flour, salt, and cayenne. Mix well. Divide mixture in half and form into 2 cheese logs (each about 1 1/2 inches in diameter and 8 inches long). Wrap each cheese log in wax paper and refrigerate overnight. **NOTE:** These can be frozen at this stage; thaw in refrigerator before baking.

When ready to bake, preheat oven to 350 degrees F.

Remove from refrigerator and slice into 1/4 inch-thick wafers and top with a pecan half. Place cheese wafers on a parchment-lined baking sheet and bake for 18–20 minutes.

Baked Cheesy Corn Dip

Yield: 8–10 servings

8 ounces cream cheese, softened

½ cup sour cream

1 cup grated Parmesan cheese

½ cup grated pepper jack cheese

4 cups corn (fresh, frozen, or canned)

4 ounces diced green chiles

2 cloves garlic, minced

1 teaspoon salt

1 teaspoon pepper

1 teaspoon paprika

8 slices crispy-cooked bacon, crumbled

4 green onions, diced

This bubbling hot corn dip is full of creamy cheese and topped with crumbled bacon. It doesn't get much better than this crowd-pleasing favorite. You can kick it up a notch with the addition of hot sauce for a little more spice.

Preheat oven to 350 degrees F. In a large mixing bowl, stir together softened cream cheese with sour cream, grated cheeses, corn, green chiles, garlic, salt, pepper, and paprika. Once combined, spread into a casserole dish. Bake, uncovered, for 30 minutes. Remove from heat and top with crumbled bacon and diced green onions.

Kentucky Hot Brown Bites

Yield: 30 bites

2 tablespoons butter

2 tablespoons all-purpose flour

²/₃ cup half-and-half

¹/₃ cup grated Pecorino Romano cheese

¹/₂ teaspoon salt

1 teaspoon white pepper

1 teaspoon paprika

³/₄ cup diced roasted turkey breast

3 slices crispy-cooked bacon, crumbled

¹/₄ cup diced tomatoes

30 phyllo cups

Chopped parsley, for garnish

Made famous by The Brown Hotel in Louisville, Kentucky, in 1926, these savory bites are miniature versions of the hot, open-face turkey sandwich covered in Mornay sauce. Phyllo cups are one of my very favorite entertaining tricks. Keep them on hand in your freezer and fill them up with anything and everything from pimento cheese to hot chicken salad to create the quickest appetizers for last-minute potlucks and occasions.

Preheat oven to 325 degrees F.

In a small saucepan, melt butter then slowly whisk in flour to form a roux. Whisk in half-and-half, stirring constantly, until mixture begins to simmer, 2–3 minutes. Remove sauce from heat and stir in cheese, salt, pepper, and paprika to create the cheese sauce. Add in turkey, bacon, and tomatoes. Stir well to combine.

Place phyllo cups evenly on a baking sheet. Add filling to each cup. Bake for 8–10 minutes. Remove from oven and garnish with parsley.

Spicy Cheddar-Sausage Balls

Yield: 60 mini sausage balls (or 30 large sausage balls)

2½ cups Bisquick baking mix

1 pound hot or spicy ground pork sausage

4 cups grated sharp cheddar cheese

½ cup milk

One of the tastiest appetizers around, these cheddar-sausage balls are a staple in almost every Southern kitchen, especially around the holidays. Fill up a silver bowl or platter with them, but have backups! They'll disappear fast. We love ours made with spicy sausage, but if you're serving them to kids or nonspice lovers, opt for regular ground sausage.

Preheat oven to 350 degrees F.

Combine the Bisquick, sausage, cheese, and milk in a large bowl. Form into 1-inch balls and place on a parchment-lined baking sheet. The dough will be sticky, so use a little flour or Bisquick on your hands to help form the balls. Bake until golden brown, 20–25 minutes.

TIP: *Take the extra step to grate your own cheese for this recipe as the bagged shredded cheese can be too dry.*

Spicy Seasoned Pecans

Yield: 4 cups

¼ cup butter, melted

½ teaspoon salt

¼ teaspoon Tabasco sauce

2 tablespoons
Worcestershire sauce

4 cups pecan halves

A Southern party classic, serve up a bowl of these spicy pecans on your bar cart or sideboard. They're the perfect salty snack for parties or food gifting.

Preheat oven to 300 degrees F.

Combine butter, salt, Tabasco sauce, and Worcestershire sauce in a mixing bowl. Stir well. Add in pecan halves and stir to evenly coat. Spread pecans in a single layer on a parchment-lined baking sheet. Bake for 20 minutes. Toss or stir several times while baking. Allow to cool and store in an airtight container.

Mini Crab Cakes with Cajun Aioli

Yields: 35 crab cakes

1 pound fresh lump crab meat or 3 cans (6-ounce) lump crab meat

1 tablespoon finely chopped green onion

2 tablespoons finely chopped red bell pepper

1 tablespoon Dijon mustard

$^1/_2$ cup breadcrumbs

2 eggs, lightly beaten

$^1/_4$ teaspoon cayenne pepper

1 teaspoon Old Bay Seasoning

$^1/_2$ cup mayonnaise

Peanut oil, for frying

Cajun Aioli

Chives, for garnish

When you really want to surprise and delight your guests, these Mini Crab Cakes with Cajun Aioli will do the trick. They're surprisingly easy to make and chock-full of crab . . . the way all crab cakes should be!

Combine crab meat with onion, bell pepper, mustard, breadcrumbs, eggs, cayenne pepper, Old Bay Seasoning, and mayonnaise in a large mixing bowl. Mix together until well blended. Form into round 1 $^1/_2$-inch crab cakes and place on parchment paper until ready to fry. Heat 1 inch oil in a cast iron frying pan to 350 degrees F. Being careful not to overcrowd the pan, fry crab cakes in batches for about 3–4 minutes on each side. Remove from heat, drain on paper towels, and top with Cajun Aioli and chives.

TIP: *Create entrée-size crab cakes to serve alongside a salad for a full meal. This recipe will make roughly 8 large crab cakes.*

CAJUN AIOLI

$^1/_2$ cup mayonnaise

1 clove garlic, minced

1 teaspoon lemon juice

1 teaspoon Cajun seasoning

$^1/_2$ teaspoon Dijon mustard

CAJUN AIOLI

In a small bowl, whisk together all ingredients and keep chilled until ready to serve with mini crab cakes.

Mini Twice-Baked Potatoes

Yield: 24–28 baked potato halves

14 to 16 mini potatoes (honey gold, or similar variety)

$1/8$ cup olive oil

3 tablespoons sour cream

1 tablespoon butter, melted

$1/2$ teaspoon salt

$1/4$ teaspoon black pepper

$1/4$ cup grated cheddar cheese

$1/4$ cup cooked, crumbled bacon

1 tablespoon finely chopped chives

Hors d'oeuvres don't have to be fussy to be delicious. Take classic comfort food and scale it down to something that can be enjoyed at a party. Mini twice-baked potatoes can keep the guys happy at a Super Bowl gathering and also hold their own among fancy canapés and hors d'oeuvres at your next cocktail party. Load them up and watch your guests, kids and adults alike, gobble them up!

Preheat oven to 400 degrees F.

Wash the potatoes and dry. Toss potatoes in olive oil. Place on a parchment-lined baking sheet and bake for 20–25 minutes. Remove from the oven and allow to cool.

Slice each potato in half and very carefully scoop out the flesh, leaving a shell. Place the scooped potato in a mixing bowl and add sour cream, butter, salt, and pepper. Mix until combined. Using a small teaspoon, fill the potato shells. Sprinkle with cheese and bacon and bake for 10–12 minutes. Remove from the oven and sprinkle with chives. Serve warm.

Southern Charcuterie Board

MEATS

Bacon, country ham, summer sausage, prosciutto, salami, etc.

NUTS

Peanuts, seasoned pecans, almonds, walnuts, etc.

BREADS & CRACKERS

Biscuits, cheese wafers, breadsticks, crostini

FRUITS & VEGETABLES

Watermelon, blackberries, strawberries, figs, peaches, fried okra, pickles, tomatoes, celery

CHEESES

Pimento cheese, brie, cheddar, Parmesan, mozzarella, etc.

GARNISHES & HERBS

Rosemary, thyme, mint, florals, honey, fig jam

Charcuterie boards are one of the best ways to serve your go-to favorites and seasonal picks. Create a Southern version of this party favorite by gathering Southern staples, from seasoned pecans and pimento cheese to Georgia peaches and, of course, bacon! Style one large charcuterie board or create miniature versions with individual wooden boards (the minis make a great appetizer to a larger meal).

Find the perfect board, like a marble slab or a wooden board—even a large plate or platter will work just fine. Begin by anchoring your board with your cheeses. Then place any little bowls for items like jams, dips, and honeys. Place cured meats throughout. Fill in any open spaces with fresh fruits and vegetables. Next, add in biscuits, cheese wafers, and nuts. Place cheese knives and mini serving spoons near where they will be needed. Just before serving, tuck in fresh herbs and floral blooms as garnishes.

TIP: *There are countless ways to create charcuterie works of art for year-round entertaining. Add in colored candies for your team's colors for a game day or chocolates and heart-shaped toasts for Valentine's Day.*

Salads
& Soups

This delightful collection of crowd-pleasing first courses will take you from backyard picnics to holiday entertaining.

Southern Fried Chicken Cobb Salad

Yield: 4–6 servings

8 cups coarsely chopped lettuce (romaine or artisan blend)

2½ cups shredded or cubed cooked chicken (fried, grilled, blackened, or rotisserie chicken)

6 slices bacon, cooked and chopped

1 cup cherry tomatoes, halved

4 hard-boiled eggs, quartered

1 cup sautéed or grilled corn

⅔ cup toasted pecans, chopped

4 ounces blue cheese, crumbled (1 cup)

1 teaspoon sea salt

1 teaspoon black pepper

2 tablespoons finely chopped chives

This lovely cobb salad takes a little bit of chopping, but it's all worth it when you serve it up to friends and family. Don't miss the homemade ranch dressing!

Using a large platter or serving tray, evenly arrange lettuce. Arrange salad ingredients on top in sections and sprinkle with salt, pepper, and chives. Serve with Buttermilk Ranch Dressing.

BUTTERMILK RANCH DRESSING

¼ cup high-quality mayonnaise (such as Duke's)

½ cup sour cream

½ cup buttermilk

1 teaspoon lemon juice

1 clove garlic, minced

½ teaspoon salt

½ teaspoon black pepper

½ teaspoon onion powder

1 teaspoon dried dill

2 tablespoons finely chopped chives

1 teaspoon finely chopped parsley

To make the Buttermilk Ranch Dressing, combine all ingredients in a medium bowl and whisk well. Adjust with additional salt or pepper to taste if needed. Dressing can be stored in a covered container in the refrigerator for up to 4 days.

Mini BLT Salads

Yield: 12 salads

12 leaves lettuce (butter or romaine) or endive spears

8 slices crispy-cooked bacon, crumbled

1 cup cherry tomatoes, chopped

½ teaspoon sea salt

½ teaspoon black pepper

¼ cup diced chives

BLTs are delightful every which way you can enjoy them. We love turning them into an easy-to-serve salad that's drizzled with a delicious Greek yogurt dressing.

Rinse lettuce leaves and pat dry. Fill each lettuce leaf evenly with bacon and tomatoes. Sprinkle with sea salt and black pepper.

BLT GREEK YOGURT DRESSING

½ cup plain Greek yogurt

¼ cup mayonnaise

1 teaspoon lemon juice

1 clove garlic, minced

3 tablespoons diced chives

¼ teaspoon sea salt

¼ teaspoon black pepper

BLT GREEK YOGURT DRESSING

Whisk together ingredients in a small bowl and drizzle over salads. Finish with a sprinkling of diced chives.

TIP: *Turn your favorite salads into party-ready servings by preparing them in lettuce cups.*

Fried Green Tomato Caprese Salad

Yield: 6–8 servings

"It's difficult to think anything but pleasant thoughts while eating a homegrown tomato."—LEWIS GRIZZARD

FRIED GREEN TOMATOES

4 to 6 medium green tomatoes

1 teaspoon salt plus extra, divided

2 eggs, room temperature

1 cup self-rising cornmeal

1/2 cup all-purpose flour

1/4 teaspoon cayenne pepper

1 teaspoon black pepper

Peanut oil for frying

When all you have in your garden are firm, green tomatoes, what else do you do but salt them, batter them, and sizzle them in oil? If you've never tried fried green tomatoes, you're in for a treat. Serve them up in a layered caprese salad for a dish that's as beautiful as is it delicious.

FRIED GREEN TOMATOES

Slice tomatoes 1/3 inch thick and place on paper towels. Press the tomatoes with additional paper towels to get most of the moisture out. Sprinkle with salt, flip the tomatoes over, and then salt again. Beat the eggs in a small bowl. In another shallow bowl, combine the cornmeal, flour, cayenne, 1 teaspoon salt, and pepper.

Heat 1–2 inches oil to 350 degrees F in a large frying pan or Dutch oven. Dip the tomatoes in the egg wash and then dredge in cornmeal mixture. Fry the slices in the oil for 3–4 minutes on each side or until golden. Place on paper towels to drain and sprinkle with a little more salt.

CAPRESE SALAD

4 medium vine-ripe red tomatoes

1 pound fresh mozzarella

1 bunch fresh basil leaves

Extra virgin olive oil

Balsamic vinegar

Coarse sea salt and ground black pepper

CAPRESE SALAD

Slice tomatoes and mozzarella into 1/3-inch-thick slices. Assemble salad in a shallow wide bowl or a platter by layering alternating slices of fried green tomatoes, red tomatoes, and mozzarella slices in a circle. Scatter fresh basil leaves throughout. Drizzle with olive oil and balsamic vinegar. Sprinkle with sea salt and black pepper. Top with petite heirloom tomatoes and mini mozzarella balls for a fun serving option.

Ambrosia Salad

Yield: 8–10 servings

4 oranges, peeled and chopped

2 cups grapefruit segments, chopped

2 cups chopped fresh pineapple

¼ cup undiluted orange juice concentrate, thawed

4 tablespoons Grand Marnier (optional)

2 tablespoons powdered sugar

1 cup shredded sweetened coconut

My grandfather's ambrosia recipe is a very traditional version of this Southern fruit salad, and he wouldn't hear of changing a single thing about it. Ambrosia, meaning "immortality" in Greek and considered "the food of the gods," has been popular since the 1860s, especially around Christmastime. You can also top your ambrosia with mini marshmallows, maraschino cherries, and pecans—we won't tell!

In a large mixing bowl, combine together all ingredients. Stir well until evenly coated. Refrigerate, covered, for at least 1 hour or overnight. Serve chilled.

Potato Salad

Yield: 12–14 servings

7 medium russet potatoes

6 hard-boiled eggs

2 cups chopped celery

1/2 yellow onion, chopped

1 tablespoon salt

1 teaspoon black pepper

2 cups super sweet pickle relish, drained

1 tablespoon sugar

1 tablespoon vinegar

1 teaspoon yellow mustard

3 tablespoons mayonnaise

While you might find heavily "mayonnaised" salad recipes touted all over the South, our version of the popular potato salad cuts back on the mayo and lets the flavors shine.

Boil potatoes, skin on, in a large pot of water for 30–40 minutes or until tender. Drain the water and allow potatoes to cool.

Peel and chop the potatoes into small pieces and place in a large bowl. Chop the eggs into small pieces and add to the potatoes, along with celery and onion.

In a small bowl, mix the salt, pepper, and relish together, and then add to the potato mixture. In another bowl, mix the sugar and vinegar together, and then add mustard and mayonnaise. Stir until well blended. Add to the potato mixture and toss gently. Add a little more mayonnaise if desired. Cover and refrigerate until ready to serve.

Trio of Bean Salads

The make-ahead element of these bean salads makes them absolutely perfect for potlucks, picnics, and any on-the-go party.

Butter Bean Salad

Yield: 8 servings

3 (9-ounce) bags frozen baby butter beans

1 cup chopped celery

1 green bell pepper, finely chopped

½ cup diced red onion

½ cup mayonnaise

¼ cup sour cream

1 teaspoon salt

½ teaspoon black pepper

½ teaspoon hot sauce

1 tablespoon balsamic vinegar

4 slices bacon, cooked and crumbled

Cook butter beans according to package directions; drain and cool completely, about 20 minutes. In a large mixing bowl, mix together butter beans, celery, bell pepper, and red onion. In a separate mixing bowl, whisk together mayonnaise, sour cream, salt, black pepper, hot sauce, and balsamic vinegar. Add mayonnaise mixture to the bean salad and stir to coat evenly. Keep refrigerated and top with bacon just before serving.

Black Bean Salad

Yield: 10–12 servings

⅓ cup red wine vinegar

⅓ cup olive oil

1 teaspoon salt

½ teaspoon black pepper

3 cloves garlic, finely chopped

3 (15.5-ounce) cans black beans, drained and rinsed

1 (15.25-ounce) can white whole kernel corn, drained

1 red bell pepper, finely chopped

1 green bell pepper, finely chopped

1 yellow bell pepper, finely chopped

1 medium red onion, finely chopped

Whisk together the vinegar, olive oil, salt, pepper, and garlic. Let this mixture marinate for 30 minutes.

In a separate bowl, stir together the black beans, corn, bell peppers, and red onion. Pour the marinade over the bean mixture; stir and toss until well coated. Cover and refrigerate for at least 8 hours or overnight.

Pea Pickin' Black-Eyed Pea Salad

Yield: 6–8 servings

2 (15.8-ounce) cans black-eyed peas, drained

1 (15.25-ounce) can white whole kernel corn, drained

1 red bell pepper, finely chopped

1 orange bell pepper, finely chopped

1 teaspoon salt

½ teaspoon crushed red pepper

¼ cup white wine vinegar

¼ cup olive oil

Mix together the black-eyed peas, corn, and peppers in a mixing bowl. In a separate bowl, whisk together the salt, red pepper, vinegar, and olive oil. Pour over the bean mixture and toss until well coated. Refrigerate until ready to serve.

Summer Melon Ball Salad

Yield: 6–8 servings

1 cup undiluted orange juice concentrate, thawed

2 cups watermelon balls

2 cups cantaloupe balls

2 cups honeydew balls

Fresh mint leaf sprigs, for garnish

I love serving simple fruit salads and parfaits, but sometimes you gotta kick it up a notch! Break out your fancy champagne glasses, wine glasses, or other stemware for a pretty presentation.

In a large mixing bowl, add orange juice concentrate to watermelon, cantaloupe, and honeydew balls; toss gently until coated. Refrigerate for at least 2 hours in an airtight container. Serve in a large bowl or in individual stemmed glasses. Garnish with mint leaves.

TIP: *When buying cantaloupes, they should smell sweet or they're not worth buying. Watermelons are ripe if their bottoms are yellow, not white.*

Cheesy Baked Potato Soup

Yield: 6–8 servings

1 cup chopped onion

$^1/_2$ cup chopped celery

$^1/_2$ cup butter

1 teaspoon salt

$^1/_2$ cup all-purpose flour

3 cups chicken broth

$^1/_4$ cup white wine

3 cups grated cheddar cheese

3 to 4 potatoes, baked, peeled and cubed

While the temperatures rarely dip below 50 degrees in the South, you'd better believe that once fall hits, we throw on our scarves and sweaters and grab a hot bowl of this soup.

In a frying pan, sauté the onion and celery in the butter until onion is translucent. Add the salt and flour and stir well. In a large pot or Dutch oven, stir the onion mixture into chicken broth. Add the wine, cheese, and potatoes. Cook on low until cheese melts, and then bring to a boil, stirring constantly. Serve hot with desired toppings.

TIP: *Set up a toppings bar for any soup party. For a loaded version of this baked potato soup, we love crumbled bacon, diced chives or green onion, cheddar cheese, and sour cream.*

Entrées &
Main Dishes

*The four seasons are
different in the South.
They're onions, celery,
bell pepper, and garlic.*

Cozy Chicken Pot Pie

Yields: 6–8 servings

4 tablespoons butter

1 cup peeled and sliced
(1/4-inch-thick) carrots

1 small onion, chopped

1 1/2 cups baby portobello
mushrooms, wiped, stems
removed and quartered

1/2 cup chopped celery

2 cloves garlic, minced

1/2 cup white wine

1/3 cup all-purpose flour

4 cups chicken broth

1 cup green peas

3/4 cup whipping cream

1 teaspoon chopped fresh
rosemary

2 teaspoons chopped fresh
parsley

1 teaspoon salt

1/2 teaspoon black pepper

4 cups shredded or cubed
cooked chicken

2 sheets frozen puff pastry,
thawed

1 egg, beaten

TIP: *Instead of traditional
flowers, think outside the box and
place mini herb arrangements
(such as mint, rosemary, or basil)
at each guest's place setting. It
makes the perfect party favor,
and the fragrance of the herbs
creates a delightful atmosphere.*

*One of my favorite comforting dishes is this chicken pot pie. It's
hearty, warm, and absolutely perfect for winter parties and
dropping off to friends and neighbors. Give the presentation some
flair by making initials out of puff pastry to serve as place cards
for your guests! Hint: If you have little ones hopping around to
help in the kitchen, let them cut out shapes from the extra puff
pastry—it'll keep them busy while you prep.*

Preheat the oven to 400 degrees F. In a Dutch oven or oven-proof
pot, melt butter and sauté carrots and onion over medium heat
until tender, 5 minutes, stirring frequently. Add mushrooms and
celery. Cook for an additional 5 minutes. Stir in garlic and wine
then cook for an additional minute. Add flour and stir well. Pour
in chicken broth and bring to boil. Cook, stirring frequently, until
sauce has thickened enough to coat the back of a spoon, 5–7
minutes. Remove from heat and stir in peas, whipping cream,
rosemary, parsley, salt, pepper, and chicken.

    Roll out 1 puff pastry sheet and cut to fit top of pot. You may
also top your chicken pot pie in a lattice pattern by cutting strips
of puff pastry and assembling on top. Brush puff pastry with egg.
Bake for 40–45 minutes or until puff pastry is golden. Cover
loosely with aluminum foil if puff pastry starts to get too brown.

    If making miniature pot pies, transfer chicken pot pie filling
to individual ramekins and top with puff pastry cut to fit top of
ramekin. Bake individual pot pies for 20–25 minutes or until puff
pastry is golden.

    Roll out second sheet of puff pastry. Use 2- to 3-inch
alphabet-shaped cookie cutters to cut out the first initial of each
of your guests. Lay the puff pastry letters on a baking sheet and
brush with egg. Bake at 400 degrees F for 12–15 minutes or until
lightly golden. Before serving, place the puff pastry initial on each
individual pot pie.

Sausage Breakfast Casserole

Yield: 8 servings

6 cups 1-inch cubes Italian bread, divided

1 pound sausage, cooked and crumbled (or 16 slices cooked bacon, crumbled)

2½ cups grated extra sharp cheddar cheese

1 small onion, diced

6 eggs

2 cups milk

½ teaspoon salt

1 teaspoon ground mustard

¼ teaspoon cayenne pepper

Every Southern hostess has a fabulous breakfast casserole in her recipe box for brunch occasions. This sausage breakfast casserole is as easy as it is delicious!

Spray a 9 x 13-inch casserole dish with nonstick cooking spray. Place 4 cups bread cubes in the bottom of the dish. Sprinkle the cooked sausage, cheese, and onion evenly over the bread.

In a mixing bowl, whisk together eggs, milk, salt, mustard, and cayenne. Pour over the casserole. Cover and chill overnight. Remove from refrigerator, set on the counter while the oven preheats to 350 degrees F, and bake for 30–35 minutes.

TIP: *Start collecting white dishes and platters. They'll coordinate with every color scheme and holiday occasion.*

Backyard Pulled-Pork Sliders

Yield: 12–14 sliders

1 tablespoon vegetable oil

1 (3 to 4 pound) boneless pork shoulder roast, trimmed

1 cup Barbecue Sauce

1/2 cup chicken broth

1/4 cup brown sugar

1/2 cup apple cider vinegar

1 tablespoon Worcestershire sauce

1 tablespoon yellow mustard

1 tablespoon chili powder

2 cloves garlic, minced

1 small onion, diced

12 to 14 slider buns

You can feed a hungry crowd with these pulled-pork sliders or enjoy the pulled pork on its own, drizzled with Barbecue Sauce. While sliders are a casual food, I've been known to serve these up on a silver platter at a cocktail party because they're just that delicious!

Pour oil in the bottom of a slow cooker. Place pork shoulder in the slow cooker and top with Barbecue Sauce, broth, brown sugar, vinegar, Worcestershire sauce, mustard, chili powder, garlic, and onion. Cover and cook 8 hours on low or 4–5 hours on high.

Shred pork using 2 forks and serve with extra Barbecue Sauce and slider buns. For optional garnish, top pulled pork with Coleslaw (page 93), sliced pickles, and sliced red onion.

Barbecue Sauce

Yield: 2 cups

1/2 cup vinegar

1 cup ketchup

1/2 cup chopped onion

1/2 teaspoon cayenne pepper

1 tablespoon liquid smoke

1/4 cup light brown sugar

2 teaspoons dry mustard

2 tablespoons Worcestershire sauce

1/2 cup butter

Combine all ingredients in a saucepan and simmer on low heat for 30 minutes to blend flavors. Store in the refrigerator in a glass jar with a lid for up to 1 week.

Charleston Grilled Chicken

Yield: 4–6 servings

2 cups pineapple juice

1 cup sherry

½ cup soy sauce

1 tablespoon sugar

2 cloves garlic, minced

3 pounds boneless, skinless chicken

My mother was first introduced to this grilled chicken marinade at a catered cocktail party in downtown Charleston. She loved it so, but no caterer likes to part ways with a recipe. The week our family moved from Charleston to Raleigh, a letter from the caterer arrived in the mail with the recipe. Even though it's a surprisingly simple marinade, we kept it under lock and key for well over twenty years. Now we hope you will enjoy it as much as we have. P.S. It makes the best grilled chicken sandwiches.

In a mixing bowl, combine juice, sherry, soy sauce, sugar, and garlic. Pour the marinade over the chicken, cover, and refrigerate for 24 hours. Drain and throw away the liquid before cooking. The chicken can be cooked in a frying pan or grilled, and it is delicious served hot or cold.

Hot Chicken Salad

Yield: 10–12 servings

4 cups cubed cooked chicken (rotisserie chicken recommended)

3 cups chopped celery

¹/₂ cup toasted sliced almonds

3 tablespoons chopped onion

2 tablespoons lemon juice

¹/₄ teaspoon cayenne pepper

¹/₂ teaspoon salt

1¹/₂ cups mayonnaise

2 (8-ounce) cans sliced water chestnuts, drained

1 cup stuffed olives, chopped (optional)

3 cups grated sharp cheddar cheese, divided

My mother has been serving this hot chicken salad at every luncheon, baby shower, church meeting, and family gathering since the 1980s. If there's a birth or a funeral in the vicinity of my mother, one of these hot chicken salads will end up on their doorstep. She has served it in casserole dishes, in baby lettuce cups, and on toasted rolls. However you serve it, be prepared to share the recipe.

Preheat oven to 350 degrees F.

Mix all ingredients together, reserving 1 cup cheese. Pour into a 9 x 13-inch casserole dish sprayed with nonstick cooking spray. Sprinkle the remaining cheese on top. Bake for 30 minutes.

Sunday Supper Pot Roast

Yield: 6–8 servings

¼ cup olive oil

2 teaspoons salt

2 teaspoons black pepper

1 (3-pound) chuck roast

1½ cups beef broth

1 cup ketchup

2 small onions, chopped

1 clove garlic, minced

¼ cup white vinegar

¼ cup Worcestershire sauce

2 teaspoons chili powder

This country-style pot roast is the perfect Sunday supper, and it doesn't get much easier. Plus, you'll have four hours on your own while the oven does the work.

Preheat oven to 325 degrees F.

Heat olive oil in a large roasting pan or Dutch oven over medium-high heat. Salt and pepper the chuck roast and sear all sides (about 1 minute on each side).

In a mixing bowl, whisk together remaining ingredients and pour over roast. Bake, covered, for 4 hours or until tender.

Buttermilk Fried Chicken

Yields: 4–6 servings

4 cups buttermilk

1 whole chicken, cut into breasts, thighs, wings, and drumsticks

2 cups self-rising flour

1 teaspoon salt

1 teaspoon black pepper

¼ teaspoon cayenne pepper

Peanut oil for frying

Fried chicken was a staple at my grandparent's house in Palestine, Texas. We all looked forward to eating fried chicken in the formal dining room in our Sunday best. Frying chicken takes a little getting used to, but this chicken is well worth the fuss!

Pour the buttermilk into a large bowl then submerge the chicken pieces in the buttermilk. Cover bowl and place in refrigerator overnight, or at least 4 hours.

In a large shallow bowl, combine flour, salt, and peppers. Remove chicken from buttermilk and drain on paper towels. Dredge each chicken piece in the flour mixture, coating evenly.

In a deep fryer or Dutch oven, heat oil to 375 degrees F.

Carefully place the chicken into the hot oil. Fry until golden brown on all sides and a thermometer inserted inside chicken reads 165 degrees F. Large pieces of chicken may have to cook a little longer. Drain on a wire rack over a paper towel–lined baking sheet to keep chicken crispy. If you find your chicken is becoming too dark on the outside before cooking through (especially larger pieces), you can finish them by baking in the oven on a rack over an aluminum foil–lined baking sheet at 350 degrees F for 20–30 minutes.

Orange-Glazed Ham

Yield: 10–12 servings

1 (8 to 10 pound) precooked ham

¹/2 cup molasses

1 cup plus 3 tablespoons light brown sugar, divided

3 tablespoons yellow mustard

¹/2 cup orange marmalade

Though ham is commonly an Easter delicacy, my family loves to make this ham throughout the year, from our New Year's Day buffet to Christmas dinner.

Preheat oven to 300 degrees F.

Place the ham in a large roasting pan. In a small bowl, whisk together molasses and 1 cup brown sugar. Spread mixture over ham and then cover ham with aluminum foil. Cook for 1 hour. Remove ham from oven and remove aluminum foil.

In a small saucepan, stir together mustard, orange marmalade, and remaining brown sugar. Heat until well combined. Spoon marmalade mixture all over the ham and serve.

TIP: *We eat with our eyes first, so take a few minutes to garnish any platters or serving trays with fresh fruit slices and herbs.*

Game Day Chili Bread Bowls

Yield: 10–12

2 small onions, diced

4 cloves garlic, minced

1 green bell pepper, diced

2 pounds ground beef

1/3 cup chili powder

1 tablespoon ground cumin

1 tablespoon smoked paprika

1 1/2 tablespoons salt

2 jalapeños, stems removed, seeded and minced

1 (28-ounce) can diced tomatoes

1 (15-ounce) can tomato sauce

1 (15-ounce) can red kidney beans, drained and rinsed

1 (15-ounce) can pinto beans, drained and rinsed

1 (15-ounce) can black beans, drained and rinsed

1 (6-ounce) can tomato paste

10 to 12 small bread rolls

TOPPINGS BAR

Grated cheddar cheese, sour cream, diced chives or green onions, tortilla chips, diced red onion, jalapeño slices

Chili is one of the best dishes to make for feeding a large crowd, especially for game days and tailgates. Serve this in mini bread bowls and your guests will be thrilled, even if their team doesn't win.

In a large pot, sauté onion, garlic, and bell pepper over medium heat until softened, about 5 minutes. Stir in beef, crumbling with a wooden spoon and cooking until no pink remains. Add chili powder, cumin, paprika, salt, and jalapeños. Simmer for 5 minutes, stirring frequently. Stir in diced tomatoes, tomato sauce, beans, and tomato paste. Bring chili to boil over medium heat. Reduce heat to low and simmer for 2–2 1/2 hours, stirring occasionally.

Cut the top off each bread roll and hollow out the inside, leaving at least 1/2 inch of bread at the bottom. You can also press the cut-out top into the bottom of the bread bowl to keep it from soaking through. Fill the bread bowls with chili and serve with toppings.

TIP: *These mini bread bowls can be filled with any of your favorite soups as well. They're perfect with tomato basil soup topped with grated cheese, as well as the Cheesy Baked Potato Soup on page 60.*

Vegetables & Sides

Whether they're roasted, fried, stewed, or sautéed, side dishes in the South garner just as much praise as our layer cakes and pies.

Lemon-Thyme Brussels Sprouts with Bacon

Yield: 4–6 servings

1½ pounds Brussels sprouts

2 tablespoons olive oil

1 tablespoon lemon juice

1 teaspoon sea salt

1 teaspoon black pepper

1 clove garlic, minced

4 slices uncooked bacon, cut into 1-inch pieces

2 tablespoons toasted pine nuts

¼ cup shaved Parmesan cheese

1 lemon, sliced

2 teaspoons fresh thyme leaves

Even my husband was converted to Brussels sprouts after trying this lemon-thyme version with bacon.

Preheat oven to 400 degrees F.

Trim the ends of the Brussels sprouts and remove any rough outer leaves. Slice the sprouts in half from top to bottom and place in a large mixing bowl. Stir together with olive oil, lemon juice, salt, pepper, and garlic. Spread Brussels sprouts in an even layer onto a cast-iron skillet or roasting pan. Top evenly with bacon pieces. Roast for 30–35 minutes or until Brussels sprouts are crispy on the edges and the bacon is cooked, tossing once during cooking. Remove from oven and top with pine nuts and shaved Parmesan. Garnish with lemon wedges and thyme.

TIP: *Be on the lookout for mini cast iron skillets. Not only are they perfect for cooking in, but they also make charming serving pieces. The cooking time remains the same.*

Ham Hock Green Beans

Yield: 6–8 servings

2 pounds green beans

$^{1}/_{2}$ cup chopped onion

1 teaspoon salt

$^{1}/_{2}$ teaspoon black pepper

1 ham hock

4 slices bacon, cooked and crumbled

The ham hock is the secret to the flavor of these old-fashioned green beans.

Wash and string the green beans. Cut whole beans in half crosswise. Place beans in a large saucepan or pot and fill with enough water to just barely cover the beans. Add onion, salt, pepper, and ham hock. Cook over medium heat until it starts to boil, and then lower heat to low and let cook, uncovered, for about 1 hour. Before serving, remove the ham hock and top with crumbled bacon. Save some for leftovers—these beans taste even better the second day.

Grilled
Country Ham–Wrapped Asparagus

Yield: 12 asparagus bundles

6 thin slices country ham

30 to 40 asparagus spears, trimmed

2 tablespoons olive oil

12 chives (optional)

This asparagus dish will impress even the fanciest dinner party guests.

Cut each slice ham in half lengthwise to make 12 pieces. Wrap each piece of ham tightly around 3 to 4 asparagus spears. Place seam side down on an oiled grill or grill pan over medium-high heat. Grill 6–8 minutes, turning frequently. Remove from grill and, for a little extra flair, secure with a chive ribbon around the ham-wrapped asparagus bundle.

TIP: *You can also recreate these bundles with green beans, as well as swapping country ham for bacon or prosciutto.*

Crispy Fried Okra

Yield: 6–8 servings

1 pound fresh okra

1 beaten egg, room temperature

$1/2$ cup self-rising flour

1 cup self-rising cornmeal

$1/2$ teaspoon salt

$1/4$ teaspoon cayenne pepper (optional)

1 to 2 cups peanut or vegetable oil

Most people proclaim they don't like okra until they've had a chance to try fried okra. Serve it up with homemade Buttermilk Ranch Dressing (page 48) for dipping.

Wash the okra and drain. Pat with paper towels. Cut the okra into $1/2$-inch slices and discard the ends. Toss okra slices in the egg until coated. Set okra slices out evenly on paper towels. Stir together the flour, cornmeal, salt, and cayenne pepper in a shallow bowl. Dredge okra in cornmeal mixture.

Heat 1 inch of oil in a large frying pan or Dutch oven to 350 degrees F. Fry the okra until golden brown, working in small batches to allow room to cook evenly. Watch carefully so it does not burn. Drain on paper towels and season with additional salt or pepper if desired.

Sweet Potato Casserole

Yield: 10–12 servings

SWEET POTATO CASSEROLE FILLING

3 to 4 pounds sweet potatoes

1 cup sugar

$1/2$ cup butter, softened

$1/4$ cup milk

2 large eggs

1 teaspoon vanilla extract

$1/4$ teaspoon salt

PECAN STREUSEL TOPPING

6 tablespoons butter, melted

1 cup dark or light brown sugar

$1/2$ cup all-purpose flour

$1^{1}/2$ cups chopped pecans

1 teaspoon cinnamon

$1/4$ teaspoon salt

A holiday buffet mainstay, this sweet potato casserole is rich, sweet, and topped with a pecan streusel. It could double as dessert, but we all know to squeeze it on our dinner plate so we can save our dessert plate for pie.

SWEET POTATO CASSEROLE FILLING

Preheat oven to 400 degrees F.

Clean and scrub sweet potatoes. Line a baking sheet with aluminum foil. Prick sweet potatoes all over with a fork. Bake for 50–60 minutes or until tender. Allow sweet potatoes to cool then remove skins and place in a large mixing bowl. Add sugar, butter, milk, eggs, vanilla, and salt and cream together until smooth, 2–3 minutes. Transfer to a 9 x 13-inch baking dish.

PECAN STREUSEL TOPPING

In a mixing bowl, stir together butter, brown sugar, flour, pecans, cinnamon, and salt until combined.

Sprinkle the streusel topping evenly over sweet potato filling and bake for 30 minutes.

VARIATION: One side of my family always prefers mini marshmallows as a topping on their sweet potato casserole, so I often sprinkle my streusel topping in "stripes" across my baking dish and, in the last 5 minutes of baking, remove the baking dish from the oven, fill in the open stripes with mini marshmallows, and return to oven to finish. It creates a beautiful dish and keeps everyone happy!

Creamy Macaroni & Cheese

Yield: 8–10 servings

16 ounces macaroni, cavatappi, or other small pasta

¹⁄₂ cup butter

¹⁄₃ cup all-purpose flour

1 teaspoon ground white pepper

¹⁄₂ teaspoon salt

¹⁄₂ teaspoon dry mustard

1 teaspoon garlic powder

¹⁄₂ teaspoon cayenne pepper

3 cups whole milk

4 ounces medium cheddar cheese, grated

8 ounces extra sharp cheddar cheese, grated, divided

4 ounces Gruyère cheese, grated

2 tablespoons butter, melted

¹⁄₂ cup seasoned panko crumbs

Macaroni and cheese is a vegetable in our house. I can't think of one occasion—from Christmas dinner to church potlucks—where we don't serve this macaroni and cheese. I've even served it in individual cups with a toppings bar for guests, and it was a hit!

Preheat oven to 375 degrees F.

Bring a large pot of salted water to boil. Add in macaroni and cook for 9–10 minutes. Drain and set aside.

In a large pot over medium heat, melt butter. Add flour, white pepper, salt, dry mustard, garlic powder, and cayenne pepper. Whisk until smooth. Stir in milk, ¹⁄₂ cup at a time, and whisk well. Add in all cheeses (reserving 4 ounces of extra sharp cheddar for topping). Stir until smooth. Pour in pasta and stir to coat evenly.

Transfer to a 2- to 3-quart baking dish. Sprinkle with remaining extra sharp cheddar cheese. In a small bowl, whisk together melted butter and panko. Sprinkle on top of cheese and bake for 30–35 minutes.

Down South–Style Cheese Grits

Yield: 4–6 servings

2 cups chicken broth

2 cups 2 percent milk

¾ cup butter, cubed

1 teaspoon salt

1 teaspoon black pepper

1 cup uncooked old-fashioned grits

1 cup grated sharp cheddar cheese

I'm from the school of thought that says cheese makes everything better, including grits. Serve them on their own or topped with shrimp.

In a large saucepan, bring chicken broth, milk, butter, salt, and pepper to a boil. Slowly stir in grits and reduce heat to medium-low. Cover and allow to cook for 12–13 minutes (or until thickened). Be sure to stir occasionally. Stir in cheese and keep warm. Top with additional cheese if desired.

Squash Casserole

Yield: 6–8 servings

8 medium yellow squash

2 tablespoons chopped onion

1 (14.5-ounce) can chicken broth

½ (10.5-ounce) can cream of chicken soup

8 ounces sour cream

½ cup butter, melted

1 (6-ounce) box stuffing mix (plain or savory herb)

Casseroles reign supreme in the South, where squash grows abundantly. Combine the two and you have one of our very favorite dishes.

Preheat oven to 350 degrees F.

Wash the squash and cut into bite-size pieces. Stir together squash, onion, and chicken broth in a large saucepan. Add enough water to cover squash. Bring to a boil and continue to boil for 20 minutes or until squash is tender. Drain liquid and toss in the soup and sour cream, stirring until squash is coated.

Mix the butter and stuffing mix then spoon about half of the mixture into the bottom of a casserole dish. Spread the squash over the stuffing then top with the remaining stuffing. Cover dish with aluminum foil. Bake for 20 minutes, uncover, and bake for 5 more minutes.

Slow-Cooked Baked Beans

Yield: 6–8 servings

2 (16-ounce) cans pork and beans

6 tablespoons light brown sugar

4 tablespoons dark corn syrup

1 teaspoon ground mustard

¾ cup ketchup

¼ cup chopped onion

3 slices uncooked bacon

1 (6-ounce) can French-fried onions (optional)

Cooked low and slow, these baked beans will be a great take-along to any barbecue gathering.

Preheat oven to 300 degrees F.

In a large mixing bowl, mix together beans, brown sugar, corn syrup, mustard, ketchup, and onion. Pour into a casserole dish and top with bacon slices. Bake for 2 hours. If desired, top with French-fried onions before serving.

Coleslaw

Yield: 8 servings

1 small head green cabbage, shredded

1 small head purple cabbage, shredded

1 medium onion, finely chopped

1 carrot, finely grated

⅓ cup white vinegar

⅓ cup mayonnaise

1 teaspoon ground mustard

1 teaspoon celery seed

1 teaspoon salt

Serve up this coleslaw on Backyard Pulled-Pork Sliders (page 68) or on its own with sliced homegrown tomatoes.

Combine cabbages, onion, and carrot in a mixing bowl. In a small bowl, stir together vinegar, mayonnaise, mustard, celery seed, and salt until well mixed. Pour dressing over slaw and toss. Refrigerate until ready to serve.

Summer Succotash

Yield: 6–8 servings

1 tablespoon extra virgin olive oil

1½ cups sliced okra

1 small onion, chopped

3 cups cooked corn

3 cups cherry tomatoes, halved

1½ cups baby lima beans

1 tablespoon salt

2 teaspoons black pepper

1 tablespoon red wine vinegar

Crumbled cooked bacon, thyme, and basil, for garnish (optional)

Bursting with summer flavors and a rainbow of colors, this easy side dish is perfect for pairing with fried chicken or pork.

In a frying pan, add olive oil and okra and cook for 10 minutes over medium heat. Stir in onion and continue to cook for 7–10 minutes until okra is tender, stirring frequently.

In a large mixing bowl, combine cooked corn, tomatoes, lima beans, and okra mixture. Sprinkle with salt, pepper, and red wine vinegar. Toss until vegetables are well coated. Refrigerate until ready to serve.

Breads

*Nothing warms the heart like
biscuits and cornbread,
so please pass the bread basket!*

Classic Southern Biscuits

Yield: 12–14 biscuits

2¹/2 cups all-purpose flour

1 tablespoon sugar

1 tablespoon baking powder

1 teaspoon salt

¹/4 cup butter, room temperature

¹/3 cup shortening

1 cup whole milk

Melted butter to brush the tops of the biscuits

Serve these biscuits at your next brunch gathering and they'll disappear faster than a hot knife through butter. They're the bread of the South for a reason. Fill them with sliced ham for Easter brunch, Nashville Hot Chicken (page 18) for game day, or a slather of Poppie's Fig Jam (page 26) and butter on Sunday morning. Play around with various biscuit cutter sizes (good ol' cookie cutters work well, too) to make bite-size versions of your favorite sandwiches.

Preheat oven to 450 degrees F.

Mix flour, sugar, baking powder, and salt until blended. Add the butter and shortening. Using a fork, work the butter and shortening into the flour mixture. Pour in milk and knead biscuits 4–5 times. Turn dough out onto a lightly floured surface. Roll dough to 1-inch thickness and cut with a biscuit cutter. Press the cutter into the dough and pull straight up—do not twist the cutter. Place biscuits on a baking sheet lined with parchment paper and bake 12–14 minutes or until lightly golden. Remove from the oven and brush with melted butter.

Louisiana Hush Puppies
with Comeback Dipping Sauce

Yield: 36 hush puppies

This Gulf Coast favorite will have your guests coming back for more.

COMEBACK DIPPING SAUCE

**COMEBACK
DIPPING SAUCE**

1 cup mayonnaise

1/3 cup ketchup

1/2 teaspoon Worcestershire sauce

1 teaspoon hot sauce

1/2 teaspoon garlic powder

1/2 teaspoon black pepper

1/2 teaspoon paprika

Stir together mayonnaise, ketchup, Worcestershire sauce, hot sauce, garlic powder, black pepper, and paprika. Set aside.

LOUISIANA HUSH PUPPIES

LOUISIANA HUSH PUPPIES

2 cups yellow cornmeal

1 tablespoon baking powder

1 teaspoon salt

1/2 teaspoon sugar

2 beaten eggs, room temperature

1 cup finely chopped onion

1 1/4 cups buttermilk

Peanut oil, for frying

Combine cornmeal, baking powder, salt, and sugar in a large mixing bowl. Stir in eggs and onion. Add in 1 cup of buttermilk and combine. Mixture should be thick enough to drop by the spoonful. Add additional 1/4 cup buttermilk if needed.

Heat 2 inches of peanut oil in a cast iron frying pan or Dutch oven to 350 degrees F. Drop batter by the spoonful and fry for 2–3 minutes on each side. Drain on paper towels. Serve with Comeback Dipping Sauce.

Southern Spoon Bread

Yield: 6–8 servings

4 large eggs, separated

¾ cup yellow cornmeal

1 tablespoon sugar

1 teaspoon salt

¼ teaspoon cayenne pepper

2 cups whole milk

¼ cup unsalted butter

It wasn't until I was in college that I discovered that spoon bread wasn't a common addition to the dinner table. We've introduced many a friend to this Southern dish, also known as "batter bread," over the years.

Preheat oven to 375 degrees F.

Using an electric mixer, beat egg whites until they form stiff peaks. Set aside. Mix together cornmeal, sugar, salt, and cayenne pepper in a large saucepan. Add in milk and cook over medium heat, stirring constantly, until thickened. Remove from stove top and stir in butter until mixture is smooth.

Beat egg yolks and gradually stir into the hot cornmeal mixture. Carefully fold in egg whites. Pour into a greased 1 ½-quart casserole dish. Bake for 30–35 minutes. Spoon bread should be puffed and golden. Remove from oven and serve immediately.

Buttermilk Skillet Cornbread

Yield: 6–8 servings

"The best comfort food will always be greens, cornbread, and fried chicken."
—MAYA ANGELOU

½ teaspoon baking soda

1½ cups buttermilk

1¾ cups yellow cornmeal

½ cup all-purpose flour

1 teaspoon salt

3 tablespoons sugar

1½ teaspoons baking powder

½ cup sour cream

2 beaten eggs, room temperature

½ cup butter, melted plus 1 tablespoon butter to grease skillet

Butter, honey, or molasses, to serve

We don't argue with Maya. Thank goodness we live in a world with buttermilk skillet cornbread. Top it with a slather of butter and a drizzle of honey.

Preheat the oven to 425 degrees F.

In a mixing bowl, combine baking soda and buttermilk. In a separate bowl, combine cornmeal, flour, salt, sugar, and baking powder. Stir in buttermilk mixture, sour cream, eggs, and butter to the dry mixture until blended, but do not overmix. Add 1 tablespoon butter into a 10-inch cast iron skillet, or 5-inch skillets, and place into the oven for about 5 minutes to heat the skillet. Carefully remove skillet then pour the cornbread batter into the hot, buttered skillet and bake 20–25 minutes. Cut into wedges and serve with butter, honey, or molasses.

Thanksgiving Dressing

Yield: 10–12 servings

6 cornbread slices or muffins

4 biscuits

1 cup finely chopped celery

1½ cups finely chopped white onions

3 eggs, room temperature, lightly beaten

1 teaspoon salt

½ teaspoon black pepper

2 cups chicken broth

My grandmother, "Sweet," was known for her Thanksgiving dressing. Even when we're away from home on Thanksgiving, my mother will make this dressing, wrap it up, freeze it, and haul it with us wherever we go.

Preheat oven to 350 degrees F.

Crumble together cornbread and biscuits into a large bowl. Stir in the celery, onion, and eggs. Add in salt and pepper and stir to combine. Add 1 cup of chicken broth at a time and stir well. Consistency should be thick. Spoon into a 9 x 13-inch casserole dish. You can freeze at this stage until ready to bake. Bake for 55–60 minutes or until lightly golden on top. Cut into squares and serve.

Blueberry Banana Bread

Yield: 10–12 slices

½ cup butter, room
temperature

1 cup sugar

2 eggs

1 tablespoon vanilla extract

2 ripe bananas, mashed

2 cups plus 1 tablespoon all-
purpose flour, divided

1 teaspoon baking soda

1 teaspoon baking powder

½ teaspoon salt

2½ cups blueberries

*Our favorite quick-to-make bread, this Blueberry Banana Bread is
a delicious addition to any brunch table and a great bake-and-
take treat for neighbors.*

Preheat oven to 350 degrees F.

In the bowl of a stand mixer, cream together butter and sugar
until light and fluffy. Add eggs, 1 at a time, and mix until combined.
Beat in vanilla. Add bananas to bowl, mixing until combined.

In a medium bowl, combine 2 cups of flour, baking soda,
baking powder, and salt. Stir until combined. Slowly add dry
ingredients to banana mixture until just combined. Don't overmix.

Toss blueberries in remaining flour until lightly coated and
stir gently into the batter. Pour batter into loaf pan sprayed with
nonstick cooking spray or lined with parchment paper. Bake
55–60 minutes or until a toothpick inserted into bread comes out
clean. Ovens vary, so watch carefully. Allow to cool completely on a
wire rack and enjoy.

Phronsie's Banana Muffins

Yield: 12 muffins

½ cup butter, room temperature

1 cup sugar

2 large eggs

3 very ripe bananas, mashed

1 teaspoon vanilla extract

½ teaspoon lemon juice

1½ cups all-purpose flour

1 teaspoon baking soda

2 tablespoons hot water

The secret to my daughter's heart, these banana muffins have become a weekly morning tradition in our house.

Preheat oven to 400 degrees F.

Cream together butter and sugar with paddle attachment of a stand mixer. Add eggs, 1 at a time, and blend well with butter and sugar. Fold in the bananas, vanilla, and lemon juice.

In a separate bowl, sift together flour and baking soda. Add to wet batter then pour in hot water. Gently fold until incorporated—do not overbeat the batter. Spoon batter into muffin tins sprayed with nonstick cooking spray. Bake 12–15 minutes.

Sunday Morning Cinnamon Rolls

Yield: 8–10 servings

$^1/_3$ cup warm water (100 degrees F)

1 tablespoon (1 packet) rapid-rise yeast

1 tablespoon sugar

$^1/_4$ cup butter, melted

$^1/_4$ cup sugar

$^1/_4$ cup warm milk

$^1/_2$ teaspoon salt

1 egg, beaten

$2^1/_4$ to $2^1/_2$ cups all-purpose flour

1 cup light brown sugar

$^1/_2$ cup butter, softened

1 teaspoon vanilla extract

$^1/_4$ teaspoon almond extract

$2^1/_2$ tablespoons cinnamon

A busy hostess rarely has time for making homemade cinnamon rolls. This delicious one-hour version will have your brunch guests oohing and aahing for more.

In a small bowl, combine warm water with yeast and 1 tablespoon of sugar. Stir and cover with a paper towel. Set aside for 5–10 minutes. Yeast will become bubbly.

In a large mixing bowl, stir together butter, sugar, milk, and salt. Add the yeast mixture and stir until combined. Mix in egg. Add 1 cup of flour, stir well, then add second cup of flour. Mix well then add remaining $^1/_4$ cup of flour. Knead dough either with hands or dough hook of stand mixer for 1–2 minutes or until dough pulls away from sides of bowl to form a soft ball. Add additional flour if dough is too sticky. Cover dough with a damp towel and set in a warm spot. If you don't have a warm spot, heat oven to 200 degrees F and place bowl inside oven with door ajar. Allow dough to rise for 20–25 minutes.

While dough is rising, mix together brown sugar, butter, extracts, and cinnamon in a small bowl to make a thick filling.

Uncover dough and punch down. Place the dough onto a floured surface and roll into a 12 x 16-inch rectangle.

Preheat oven to 350 degrees F. Spread filling evenly over the entire surface of the dough. You may need to use the back of a wooden spoon to press it down evenly. Starting on the long side, gently roll the dough into a log shape and slice dough gently into $1^1/_2$-inch cinnamon rolls. Prepare dish or baking sheet by buttering or spraying with nonstick cooking spray. Place the rolls into dish or space them evenly on baking sheet. Cover with plastic wrap and allow rolls to rise again for 15 minutes. Bake for 20–22 minutes or until lightly golden.

VANILLA GLAZE

1½ cups powdered sugar

½ teaspoon vanilla extract

¼ teaspoon almond extract

¼ cup butter, melted

2 tablespoons milk

VANILLA GLAZE

Whisk together powdered sugar, extracts, butter, and milk until smooth. For a thicker glaze, add more powdered sugar. For a thinner glaze, add more milk. Remove cinnamon rolls from oven and spread frosting on top.

TIP: *Instead of larger cinnamon rolls, cut rectangle of dough in half. Roll and slice mini cinnamon rolls. These bite-size versions are perfect for serving at a stand-up gathering.*

Cookies
& Candies

*There's no sugar coatin'
it, these bite-size treats
are just heavenly.*

Chocolate Chunk Pecan Cookies

Yield: 18 cookies

1½ cups all-purpose flour

½ teaspoon salt

½ teaspoon baking soda

¼ teaspoon ground cinnamon

½ cup unsalted butter, room temperature

½ cup firmly packed dark brown sugar

¼ cup sugar

1 large egg, room temperature

1 teaspoon vanilla extract

2 cups semisweet chocolate chunks (or chips)

1 cup chopped pecans

Sea salt for sprinkling on top, optional

As a hostess, I always love to find clever ways to elevate classic favorites like chocolate chip cookies. Chocolate chunks and pecans make this an over-the-top cookie worthy of any silver platter. Tuck in a few extra floral blooms for the prettiest of presentations.

Preheat oven to 375 degrees F. Line a baking sheet with parchment paper and set aside.

In a large bowl, combine flour, salt, baking soda, and cinnamon. Set aside. Using a stand mixer with paddle attachment, cream together butter and sugars until light and fluffy, 2–3 minutes. Add in egg and vanilla and beat again for 1 minute. Add in flour mixture in 2 batches and stir together with a spatula or wooden spoon, until fully mixed. Fold in chocolate chunks and pecans.

Scoop 2 tablespoons of dough and roll into a ball. Gently press with your hand and place on parchment-lined baking sheet. Be sure to leave at least 2 inches between each cookie. Sprinkle with sea salt if using. Bake for 10–12 minutes or until edges are golden. Cookies will keep in an airtight container for up to 4 days. These cookies also freeze well.

TIP: *Shiny baking sheets and cake pans are best. Dark coated pans absorb more heat and can cause cookies to overbrown.*

Cream Cheese Cookies

Yield: 24 cookies

½ cup butter, softened

4 ounces cream cheese, room temperature

1 cup sugar

1 egg, room temperature

1 teaspoon vanilla extract

1 teaspoon almond extract

½ teaspoon baking powder

1¾ cups cake flour

There is no comparison to these pillowy soft cream cheese cookies. They're a charming little bite, perfect for enjoying with coffee or tea.

Cream together butter and cream cheese with a stand mixer. Add sugar and beat for 1 minute. Add egg and beat to combine. Next, add extracts and beat until combined. Add in baking powder and cake flour (in 3 parts), mixing to combine. Once incorporated, refrigerate dough for at least 1 hour.

Preheat oven to 375 degrees F.

Line a baking sheet with parchment paper.

Dough will be sticky, so use flour on your hands to roll out 1- to 2-inch balls. You can use the bottom of a cup or glass dipped in flour to gently flatten the balls. Don't flatten too much or the cookies won't puff up. Bake 9–11 minutes. Pull the cookies out of the oven when you see the underside edges turning golden. This might vary for your oven and altitude. Watch carefully.

Kentucky Bourbon Balls

Yield: 36 bourbon balls

2¹/2 cups vanilla wafer crumbs, approximately 1 (11-ounce) box

2 tablespoons cocoa powder

1¹/2 cups powdered sugar, divided

¹/2 teaspoon salt

1 cup finely chopped pecans

3¹/2 tablespoons white corn syrup

¹/4 cup plus 2 tablespoons bourbon

This no-bake candy is easy to make and adds the perfect sweet and slightly boozy addition to any holiday cookie platter.

Combine vanilla wafer crumbs, cocoa powder, 1 cup powdered sugar, salt, and pecans in a mixing bowl. Stir together well. Add in corn syrup and bourbon, mixing well. Shape mixture into 1-inch balls and roll in remaining powdered sugar. Keep in a metal tin or airtight container for at least 12 hours or overnight until serving. Some powdered sugar will soak into bourbon balls, enhancing their flavor, but you can also roll them in additional powdered sugar before serving.

Snowball Pecan Cookies recipe on page 120.

Snowball Pecan Cookies

Yield: 30–34 cookies

3/4 cup butter, melted

5 tablespoons sugar

2 cups cake flour

1 teaspoon vanilla extract

1 teaspoon ice cold water

1/2 cup chopped pecans

1 cup powdered sugar

My mother could always tell who'd gotten into the can of Snowball Pecan Cookies by way of the powdered sugar dusted all over our clothes. They're worth it, and I also happen to think they make every platter prettier.

Preheat oven to 350 degrees F.

Cream together butter and sugar until light and fluffy, using a stand mixer. Add in the flour, vanilla, and water. Mix until well blended. Stir in pecans and form dough into small 1-inch balls and place on a parchment-lined baking sheet. Bake for 15 minutes. Cookies will be light colored and slightly golden on the bottom. Allow to cool then roll in powdered sugar.

Photo on page 119.

Creamy Peanut Butter Fudge

Yield: 50–60 squares

3 cups sugar

1 cup whole milk

3 teaspoons cornstarch

1/2 teaspoon salt

1/4 cup unsalted butter, melted

1 teaspoon vanilla extract

1 1/2 cups creamy peanut butter

If you love peanut butter, then you will quickly find that this peanut butter fudge is your new favorite treat! Gift it to neighbors, friends, and family during the holidays.

Combine the sugar, milk, cornstarch, and salt in a medium saucepan over medium heat. Bring mixture to a boil, stirring continuously. Once a rolling boil is reached, allow to continue boiling for 6 minutes, stirring frequently. Remove from the stove and stir in butter, vanilla, and peanut butter until well combined. Working quickly, pour mixture into an 8 x 8-inch pan lined with parchment paper. After cooled and set, cut into 1-inch squares.

Photo on page 122.

Fabulous Chocolate Fudge

Yield: 100 squares

4½ cups sugar

1 (12-ounce) can evaporated milk

4 teaspoons cornstarch

3 cups semisweet chocolate chips

1 cup unsalted butter, room temperature

3 tablespoons vanilla extract

1½ cups toasted chopped pecans (optional)

My godmother, Jayne, shared her recipe for chocolate fudge with me, which was passed down from her grandmother. We gift it to neighbors and friends each year and serve it at our annual Gingerbread House Tea Party. It's a holiday staple. And you read it right: three full tablespoons of vanilla extract.

Combine the sugar, milk, and cornstarch in a large saucepan over medium heat. Bring mixture to a boil, stirring continuously. Once a rolling boil is reached, allow to continue boiling for 6 minutes, stirring frequently. Remove from the stove and stir in chocolate chips, butter, and vanilla until well combined. If adding pecans, add them now and stir well. Quickly spread mixture onto a 9 x 13-inch pan lined with parchment paper and allow to cool. After fudge has cooled, lift out of pan using the ends of parchment paper and cut into 1-inch squares.

TIP: *Place fudge squares in foil candy wrappers for a pretty presentation.*

Creamy Peanut Butter Fudge recipe on page 121.

Creamy Pecan Pralines

Yield: 45–50 pralines

1¹/2 cups sugar

1¹/2 cups packed light
brown sugar

1 cup heavy cream

¹/2 teaspoon cream of tartar

¹/4 teaspoon salt

3 cups toasted pecan halves

¹/2 cup unsalted butter

2 teaspoons vanilla extract

These New Orleans–style pralines are creamy and full of pecan flavor. It's easy to see why they've earned the top spot as the South's most iconic candy.

Combine the sugars, cream, cream of tartar, and salt in a heavy saucepan and bring to a rolling boil over medium heat, stirring constantly. Continue to stir constantly, and after 15 minutes, place a candy thermometer in the pan and watch until the mixture reaches 240 degrees F (a firm softball stage, similar in texture to a soft caramel candy). Remove from heat and add the pecans, butter, and vanilla. Stir vigorously with a wooden spoon until it becomes creamy and starts to thicken. This may take 2–3 minutes. Spoon the candy quickly onto parchment-lined baking sheets. Cool and store candy between layers of parchment in an airtight container.

Easy Saltine Pecan Toffee

Yield: 30 toffee pieces

35 to 40 saltine crackers (approximately 2 sleeves)

1 cup unsalted butter

1 cup dark brown sugar

2 cups semisweet chocolate chips

1 cup chopped pecans

Bless your heart if you've ever stood over a copper pot stirring 'til your arm falls off all while trying to reach a certain temperature on your thermometer so you can have "official" English toffee. If you're hosting a party, you have no time for that, so let me let you in on a little secret: this Easy Saltine Pecan Toffee tastes just as good and you can whip it together in minutes.

Preheat oven to 400 degrees F. Line a baking sheet with parchment paper sprayed with nonstick cooking spray. Arrange crackers in a single layer, covering baking sheet.

In a saucepan, combine butter and sugar. Stirring frequently, bring to a boil for 3 minutes. Remove from heat and immediately pour over saltines, spreading to edges to evenly coat. Bake for 5–6 minutes. Remove from oven and sprinkle with chocolate chips. Allow to cool on the counter for 5 minutes then spread the chocolate chips evenly across toffee. Top with chopped pecans and allow to cool completely before breaking into toffee pieces.

TIP: *This toffee is an easy make-ahead item. Always try to have a few recipes from your party menu that can be prepped at least one day before your gathering.*

Southern Almond Tea Cakes

Yield: 12 large tea cakes

1¹/3 cup sugar

4 ounces almond paste

1 cup plus 2 tablespoons butter-flavored Crisco shortening

2 eggs plus 1 egg yolk

1 teaspoon vanilla extract

4 teaspoons almond extract

3¹/2 cups all-purpose flour

2 tablespoons cornstarch

1 teaspoon baking powder

1 teaspoon salt

¹/4 cup buttermilk

I was first introduced to almond tea cakes in my Chi Omega sorority house during my freshman year at Vanderbilt University. They came from a local Tennessee bakery, Ham'n Goodys. When I delivered my daughter, Blakely, I told my husband the first treat I wanted after her birth was a box of tea cakes. I've been on a mission to create a recipe for them for more than a decade. Ham'n Goodys' recipe might be a guarded secret, but I'm pretty proud of my version.

Preheat oven to 350 degrees F. and line a baking sheet with parchment paper.

Using a food processor, pulse the sugar with almond paste until well combined. Transfer sugar mixture to the bowl of a stand mixer with paddle attachment. Cream together sugar mixture with 1 cup shortening until light and fluffy. Add in eggs, 1 at a time. Add in extracts. Cream together for 1–2 minutes until light and fluffy. In a separate mixing bowl, combine flour, cornstarch, baking powder, and salt. Stir well. Add flour mixture and buttermilk, alternating between them, until a sticky dough is formed.

Flour a working surface. Flour hands and pat dough down flat to about ¹/2-inch thickness. Dough will be sticky, so add a sprinkling of flour whenever needed. Using a 4-inch round cookie cutter or biscuit cutter dipped in flour, cut out large round circles of the thick dough. Lift dough circles up carefully and place on baking sheet. Melt remaining shortening and brush over unbaked tea cakes. Bake 14–16 minutes. Tea cakes stay relatively light in color as opposed to golden brown, so check for doneness by carefully lifting up to see if bottom is set. Be careful not to overbake. Allow to cool before glazing.

NOTE: *You can substitute butter for the butter-flavored shortening, but in my experience, the shortening creates a tea cake closest to the original.*

ALMOND GLAZE

3½ cups sifted powdered sugar

2 teaspoons almond extract

4 to 5 tablespoons milk or heavy whipping cream

ALMOND GLAZE

Whisk together powdered sugar, almond extract, and milk until smooth. If glaze is too thick, add additional milk, but be careful not to make the glaze runny. Use a spoon to spread glaze evenly over the tops of the tea cakes. Allow glaze to set for at least 15 minutes before serving. Tea cakes can be stored in an airtight container for up to 5 days.

Cakes & Desserts

Even Southern babies know that "Gimme some sugar"
is not a request for the granular substance that
sits in a pretty bowl in the middle of the table.

Summertime Peach Shortcakes

Yield: 8 shortcakes

$^1/_2$ cup unsalted butter, melted

1 (16-ounce) box pound cake mix

4 eggs, room temperature, divided

8 ounces cream cheese, softened

3 cups powdered sugar

2 cups whipped cream

3 peaches, sliced

Fresh mint sprigs, for garnish

In the South, we count our blessings, not our carbs. We love to top these shortcakes with every type of fresh fruit, from peaches and strawberries to blackberries and cherries.

Preheat oven to 350 degrees F.

Line a 9 x 13-inch jelly roll or similar baking pan with sides with parchment paper.

With a stand mixer, cream together butter, cake mix, and 2 eggs. The batter will be thick. Press the batter evenly into prepared pan. In a mixing bowl, beat cream cheese, remaining 2 eggs, and powdered sugar for 2–3 minutes, until light and fluffy. Spread over cake mixture, being sure to spread evenly to the edges of the pan.

Bake for 35–40 minutes or until lightly golden. Allow to cool and cut into $3^1/_2$–inch circles with a cookie cutter or biscuit cutter. You can also cut them into squares or other shapes. Top each shortcake with a dollop of whipped cream, sliced peaches, and a sprig of fresh mint.

TIP: *These shortcakes are a great make-ahead dessert. Bake the shortcake circles the day before your party and keep in an airtight container in the refrigerator. Remove and top with fresh fruit before serving.*

Mama Jean's Banana Pudding

Yield: 6–8 servings

1 cup sugar

⅓ cup all-purpose flour

2 cups whole milk

3 egg yolks, beaten

2 tablespoons butter

2 teaspoons vanilla extract

4 ripe bananas, sliced

1 (11-ounce) box vanilla
wafer cookies

I've been hearing about Mama Jean's banana pudding since the day I married my husband. His grandmother was famous for this Southern delight, and my mother-in-law was tickled pink for me to share it with all of you. You can top it with a baked meringue topping or a simple swirl of whipped cream.

In a large saucepan, add sugar to flour and mix well. Gradually add milk. Place saucepan on stove and cook over medium heat, stirring constantly. When heated well, add egg yolks. Cook until thickened and remove from stove. Immediately stir in butter and vanilla. Immediately stir in butter and vanilla. If serving in individual portions, as shown, layer each serving dish with pudding, banana slices, and vanilla wafer cookies. Top with whipped cream and keep chilled until ready to serve. For a baked meringue topping, layer pudding with banana slices and vanilla wafer cookies in an 8–10-inch oven-safe baking dish. Top with Meringue Topping.

MERINGUE TOPPING

3 egg whites

¼ cup sugar

½ teaspoon vanilla extract

MERINGUE TOPPING

Preheat oven to 400 degrees F.

Beat egg whites until stiff peaks form. Add sugar and vanilla. Spread over banana pudding and bake for 5–6 minutes or until lightly browned on top.

Caramel Celebration Cake

Yield: 10–12 servings

4 cups cake flour

1 teaspoon baking soda

2 teaspoons baking powder

1 teaspoon salt

2¼ cups sugar

½ cup vegetable oil

1 cup butter

1½ tablespoons vanilla extract

3 whole eggs plus 2 egg yolks

2¼ cups buttermilk

CARAMEL ICING

½ cup butter

1 cup brown sugar

¼ cup milk

2 cups sifted powdered sugar

½ teaspoon vanilla extract

1 pinch salt

TIP: *Caramel icing is long known to be difficult, even for the most accomplished bakers. The key is to work quickly and spread the icing before it sets up.*

My mother always made birthdays a big to-do in our family, with balloons hanging from the chandelier and the most gorgeous birthday cakes on crystal cake stands. This caramel cake is certainly celebration worthy!

Preheat oven to 325 degrees F. Prepare 3 (8-inch) round cake pans by spraying with nonstick baking spray and lining with parchment paper cut rounds to fit bottom of cake pan.

Sift cake flour, baking soda, baking powder, and salt into a mixing bowl; set aside. With a stand mixer, cream together sugar, vegetable oil, butter, and vanilla. Beat well at medium-high speed until light and fluffy. Beat the 3 whole eggs in, 1 at a time, then add in the 2 egg yolks.

Fold in the dry ingredients alternately with buttermilk, beginning and ending with dry ingredients. Do not overmix the batter. Batter will be thick. Evenly divide batter between prepared pans and bake for 30–35 minutes or until toothpick inserted comes out clean. Allow cake to cool 10 minutes before turning onto wire racks to cool completely.

CARAMEL ICING

Melt butter and brown sugar together in a saucepan over medium-low heat. Add milk and bring to a boil, stirring constantly. Remove from heat and whisk in powdered sugar, 1 cup at a time. Using a hand-held mixer helps to smooth the icing. Add vanilla and salt. Add more powdered sugar for a thicker icing, if desired. As icing cools, it will set, so work quickly to pour and then spread icing over cake. This icing also works well for a sheet cake. If icing begins to set up, warm slightly in the microwave to make icing more spreadable. **NOTE:** This will be a thin layer of icing on the cake. If you want a thick layer, double the icing recipe. For layer cakes, lay sheets of wax paper around the cake as you spread on the icing to catch any overflow.

Old-Fashioned Coconut Cake

Yield: 10–12 servings

2 cups sugar

$1/2$ cup butter, softened

$1/2$ cup coconut oil

5 eggs, separated

$2^{1}/4$ cups cake flour

1 teaspoon baking powder

$1/2$ teaspoon baking soda

$1/4$ teaspoon salt

1 cup sour cream

$1^{1}/2$ cups sweetened shredded coconut

1 teaspoon coconut extract

$1/2$ teaspoon vanilla extract

$1/2$ teaspoon almond extract

$1/4$ teaspoon cream of tartar

Two ingredients are dear to any Southerner's heart: butter and sugar. Add in coconut and you have one of the best desserts around.

Preheat oven to 325 degrees F. Prepare 3 (9-inch) round cake pans with nonstick cooking spray.

In a large bowl, beat together sugar, butter, and oil until well blended. Add egg yolks, 1 at a time, beating well after each addition.

In a separate bowl, combine flour, baking powder, baking soda, and salt. Add dry ingredients to butter mixture, alternating with sour cream. Add in coconut and extracts. In the bowl of a stand mixer, use a clean whisk to beat cream of tartar with egg whites at medium speed until stiff peaks form. Fold $1/4$ of egg whites into cake batter then carefully fold in the remaining egg whites. Do not overmix. Evenly divide cake batter between baking pans. Bake for 25–30 minutes or until toothpick inserted comes out clean. Allow cake to cool 10 minutes before turning onto wire racks to cool completely.

COCONUT FROSTING

8 ounces cream cheese, softened

$1/2$ cup butter, softened

3 to 4 cups powdered sugar

$1^{1}/2$ teaspoons coconut extract

2 cups sweetened shredded coconut

COCONUT FROSTING

Beat together cream cheese and butter with a stand or hand mixer until light and fluffy. Add powdered sugar, 1 cup at a time, until desired consistency is reached. Frosting should be light and fluffy. Add in coconut extract and beat for 2–3 minutes. Frost cooled cake layers and top with shredded coconut. **NOTE:** To make a finer shredded coconut, pulse it for 15 seconds in a food processor.

Sour Cream Pound Cake

Yield: 12 servings

1 1/2 cups butter, room temperature

1/2 cup Crisco shortening

3 cups sugar

1 1/2 cups sour cream

3 cups all-purpose flour

2 teaspoons baking powder

6 eggs, room temperature

1/2 cup whole milk

2 teaspoons vanilla extract

When I was growing up, there wasn't a church gathering that didn't include a lace-topped tablecloth lined with pound cakes. Everyone has their own favorite pound cake recipe, and this one is ours. We love it topped with vanilla glaze, fresh fruit slices, or served on its own.

Preheat oven to 325 degrees F. Prepare a Bundt pan with nonstick cooking spray or greased with shortening and lightly floured.

Using a stand mixer, cream together butter and shortening. Add in sugar and sour cream. Beat until light and fluffy, about 2 minutes. In a separate mixing bowl, combine flour and baking powder. In another bowl, whisk together eggs, milk, and vanilla. Alternate adding the wet and dry mixtures to creamed butter, beating after each addition until combined. Pour batter into prepared Bundt pan. Bake for 80–90 minutes or until toothpick inserted comes out clean. Be sure not to overbake. Allow cake to cool at least 20 minutes before running a knife around sides of pan and flipping over onto a cake plate.

TIP: *When measuring flour, spoon flour into measuring cup and then level using the straight edge of a knife.*

POUND CAKE GLAZE

2 1/2 cups powdered sugar

3 tablespoons butter, melted

1 tablespoon milk

POUND CAKE GLAZE

Whisk together powdered sugar, butter, and milk. Drizzle glaze evenly over pound cake.

TIP: *Garnish pound cakes and other sweet treats with edible flowers (grown with no pesticides) such as geraniums, violets, roses, Sweet Williams, daisies, pansies, and even chive blossoms.*

Red Velvet Cupcakes

Yield: 24 cupcakes

1/2 cup unsalted butter, room temperature

1 1/2 cups sugar

2 eggs, room temperature

2 1/3 cups cake flour

2 tablespoons unsweetened cocoa powder

1 teaspoon baking soda

1 teaspoon baking powder

1/2 teaspoon salt

1 cup buttermilk

1 teaspoon distilled white vinegar

2 teaspoons vanilla extract

2 tablespoons red food coloring

The Waldorf Astoria Hotel in New York City claims it's the birthplace of red velvet cake, but it's widely known as a Southern recipe, especially popular at Christmas. This soft and velvety cake is a gorgeous shade of red and can be made as either a large layer cake or as cupcakes.

Preheat oven to 350 degrees F. Prepare cupcake tins with paper liners

Cream together butter and sugar with a stand mixer until light and fluffy, 2–3 minutes. Add eggs, 1 at a time, beating well after each addition. In a separate mixing bowl, stir together the flour, cocoa powder, baking soda, baking powder, and salt. In another small bowl, whisk together buttermilk, white vinegar, vanilla, and food coloring.

Add 1/3 dry ingredients to creamed mixture and beat until incorporated. Next, add 1/3 of the wet ingredients and beat. Continue alternating ingredients and beating to combine, finishing with dry ingredients. Scoop batter into cupcake liners, filling 2/3 full, and bake for 20–22 minutes or until toothpick inserted comes out clean. Allow to cool before frosting.

FLUFFY CREAM CHEESE FROSTING

8 ounces cream cheese, room temperature

1/2 cup unsalted butter

3 1/2 cups powdered sugar

1 teaspoon vanilla extract

FLUFFY CREAM CHEESE FROSTING

Beat together cream cheese and butter until light and fluffy using a stand mixer. Add powdered sugar, 1 cup at a time, scraping down sides between each addition. Add vanilla and beat for 2–3 minutes. Fill a piping bag with frosting and pipe swirls onto the cooled cupcakes.

Strawberry Cake

Yield: 10–12 servings

VANILLA ALMOND CAKE

¾ cup unsalted butter, room temperature

1¾ cup sugar

3 large eggs, room temperature

2 teaspoons almond extract

2 teaspoons vanilla extract

2½ cups all-purpose flour

2½ teaspoons baking powder

½ teaspoon salt

1¼ cups whole milk

STRAWBERRY JAM BUTTERCREAM

1 cup unsalted butter, softened

⅓ cup strawberry jam

4 to 5 cups powdered sugar

1 teaspoon vanilla extract

¼ teaspoon salt

1 drop red food coloring (optional)

1 to 2 cups strawberries

NOTE: *Recipe yields a 2-layer cake. To make an extra tall layer cake (perfect for a crowd), double the recipe and divide among either 3 baking pans (for thick layers, shown here) or 4 baking pans for a 4-layer cake.*

Southern porches have been used to entertain for years. My grandparents practically lived on their white wrap-around porch dotted with white wicker furniture and ferns. They always had a tea cart pulled up with at least one sweet treat and something cold to drink. This strawberry cake is a porch party favorite.

VANILLA ALMOND CAKE

Preheat oven to 375 degrees F. Spray 2 (8-inch) round baking pans with nonstick cooking spray or line with parchment paper rounds. In a stand mixer, cream together butter and sugar until light and fluffy, 2 minutes. Add eggs, 1 at a time, beating well after each addition. Scrape down sides of bowl and mix in extracts.

In a separate bowl, combine flour, baking powder, and salt. Add half of flour mixture to creamed mixture and beat on low until just combined. Add ½ cup milk and mix until just combined. Add remaining flour mixture and milk then mix until batter is combined. Do not overmix.

Divide batter evenly between pans and bake for 30–35 minutes or until toothpick inserted in the center comes out clean. Allow cake to cool for 10 minutes then carefully invert onto a wire rack to cool. I often freeze cake layers at this stage so they are easier to frost on the day they are needed.

STRAWBERRY JAM BUTTERCREAM

In a stand mixer, cream butter until light and fluffy. Add jam and beat until well mixed. Add powdered sugar, 1 cup at a time, until desired consistency is reached. For a thicker frosting, add additional powdered sugar. Whip in vanilla and salt. For a deeper pink color, add food coloring. Frost cooled cake layers, adding strawberries between layers, and serve.

Homemade Chocolate Brownies

Yield: 24 brownies

1 cup unsalted butter

2¼ cups sugar

4 large eggs, room temperature

2 teaspoons vanilla extract

1⅓ cups unsweetened cocoa powder

1 teaspoon salt

1½ teaspoons baking powder

1⅓ cups all-purpose flour

2 cups mini semisweet chocolate chips

Better than box mix, these homemade chocolate brownies will delight your guests, young and old.

Preheat oven to 350 degrees F. Prepare a 9 x 9-inch pan with nonstick cooking spray.

In a saucepan over low heat, melt butter. Add sugar and stir until just combined. Remove from heat and pour into heat-proof mixing bowl. Stir in eggs, 1 at a time. Add vanilla and stir until combined. Stir in cocoa powder, salt, baking powder, and flour until combined. Stir in chocolate chips. Spread brownie batter into pan and bake for 30–40 minutes or until a toothpick in the center comes out clean. Be careful not to overbake.

Lemon Squares

1 cup all-purpose flour

¼ cup powdered sugar

½ cup butter, melted

1 cup granulated sugar

½ teaspoon baking powder

¼ teaspoon salt

2 eggs, beaten

½ cup lemon juice

1 tablespoon lemon zest

2–3 tablespoons powdered sugar, for garnish

Add these lemon squares to any tea party platter and watch them disappear faster than you can say y'all!

Preheat oven to 350 degrees F. Prepare an 8 x 8-inch pan with nonstick cooking spray

Combine flour, powdered sugar, and butter in a bowl and stir well. Press into the bottom of the pan and bake for 20 minutes.

In a separate bowl, combine remaining ingredients then pour mixture on top of baked base and return to oven for 25 minutes. Allow to cool then refrigerate until chilled. Cut into squares and sprinkle with powdered sugar just before serving.

Shenandoah Valley Apple Cake

Yield: 12–14 servings

1¹⁄₂ cups vegetable oil

2 cups sugar

3 large eggs, room temperature

3 cups chopped Granny Smith apples (3 to 4 apples)

3 cups all-purpose flour

1 cup chopped pecans

3 tablespoons vanilla extract

1 teaspoon salt

1 teaspoon baking soda

1 teaspoon ground nutmeg

1 teaspoon ground cinnamon

One weekend in college, my mother and her roommates traveled to western Virginia to visit their suitemate Harriet's grandparents. This glazed apple cake was served as dessert for Sunday lunch. My mother begged Harriet's grandmother for the recipe, and she graciously shared it with all the girls.

Preheat oven to 325 degrees F. Prepare a 9 x 13-inch baking pan with nonstick cooking spray or line with parchment.

In the bowl of a stand mixer, beat oil, sugar, and eggs until well blended. Stir in apples, flour, pecans, vanilla, salt, baking soda, nutmeg, and cinnamon until combined. Pour batter into pan and bake for 45–50 minutes or until toothpick inserted comes out clean.

BROWN SUGAR GLAZE

¹⁄₂ cup butter, room temperature

1 cup light brown sugar

1 teaspoon vanilla extract

¹⁄₂ cup milk

BROWN SUGAR GLAZE

In a saucepan, bring butter, brown sugar, vanilla, and milk to a rolling boil over medium heat, stirring often. Remove from heat and pour over cooled cake. Slice into squares and serve.

Key Lime Trifles

Yield: 6 trifles

1 teaspoon key lime zest

⅓ cup key lime juice

1 (14-ounce) can sweetened condensed milk

¾ cup heavy whipping cream

6 slices pound cake

1½ cups graham cracker crumbs

1 cup whipped cream, for garnish

Key lime slices and zest, for garnish

You don't have to live in Florida to indulge in these pretty little Key Lime Trifles.

In a mixing bowl, stir together lime zest, juice, and condensed milk; set aside. In a separate bowl, beat whipping cream until soft peaks form. Fold whipped cream into lime mixture. Refrigerate until ready to use.

Cut pound cake slices into small cubes. Fill each trifle glass with a layer of graham cracker crumbs, followed by alternating layers of key lime filling (pour into a plastic bag and snip corner for easy layering) and pound cake cubes. Finish with a swirl of whipped cream, a lime slice, and zest.

TIP: *Turn any of your favorite desserts or cakes into party-ready presentation by layering them in tall glasses.*

Easy-as-Pie Ice Cream, Three Ways

You can make a totally indulgent ice cream with only three ingredients without ever having to shake salt or convince your spouse you need that massive ice cream maker. This no-churn base is creamy, delicious, and perfect for an ice cream sundae bar. It's as "easy as pie."

No-Churn Ice Cream Base

2 cups cold heavy whipping cream

1 (14-ounce) can sweetened condensed milk

1 (5-ounce) can evaporated milk

In a chilled stand mixer bowl, whip cream until thickened and firm peaks form, about 2 minutes. You don't want *stiff* peaks to form, however, or you'll end up making butter—which isn't a bad thing, but not good for this recipe. Using a rubber spatula, gently fold in the condensed milk, evaporated milk, and any mix-ins being used.

TIP: *Experiment with fruit and candy mix-ins to create your own ice cream flavors. For example, at Christmas, I add two teaspoons of peppermint extract, five drops of green food coloring, and red heart sprinkles on top to make a green Grinch ice cream for the kids.*

Peach Ice Cream

No-Churn Ice Cream Base

4 ripe peaches

Peel and slice peaches. Place 3 peaches into a blender or food processor and pulse until puréed. Chop the remaining peach. Fold the peach purée into the ice cream base and pour into an ice cream pan (or loaf pan). Place chopped peach on top, cover with a sheet of wax paper, and freeze for at least 8 hours.

Blackberry Ice Cream

No-Churn Ice Cream Base

4 cups blackberries

Pulse 3 cups blackberries in a blender or food processor until puréed. Fold the blackberry purée into the ice cream base and pour into an ice cream pan (or loaf pan). Place remaining cup of fresh blackberries on top, cover with a sheet of wax paper, and freeze for at least 8 hours.

Bourbon Pecan Chocolate Chip Ice Cream

No-Churn Ice Cream Base

1 cup semisweet chocolate chips

1 cup pecan halves, roughly chopped

2 to 3 tablespoons bourbon

Stir chocolate chips, pecans, and bourbon into ice cream base. Pour ice cream into an ice cream pan (or loaf pan), top with a sheet of wax paper, and freeze for at least 8 hours.

Overnight Coffee Cake

Yield: 12 servings

¾ cup butter, softened

1 cup sugar

1 cup sour cream

2 eggs, room temperature

2 cups all-purpose flour

1 teaspoon nutmeg

½ teaspoon salt

1 teaspoon baking soda

¾ cup packed light brown sugar

¾ cup chopped pecans

2 teaspoons cinnamon

If you have company coming, this is the perfect recipe, because you can prep it the day before they arrive and pop it in the oven for breakfast—and your house will smell amazing. This recipe is my brother David's absolute favorite.

Prepare a 9 x 13-inch pan with nonstick cooking spray.

Combine the butter, sugar, and sour cream and beat until fluffy. Add the eggs and mix well. Next, add the flour, nutmeg, salt, and baking soda to the batter and stir until well blended. Pour into the prepared pan. In a separate bowl, combine the brown sugar, pecans, and cinnamon then sprinkle over batter. Cover and chill overnight. When ready to bake, preheat oven to 350 degrees F. Bake for 35–40 minutes.

COFFEE CAKE GLAZE

1 cup powdered sugar

1 tablespoon milk

1 tablespoon butter, melted

½ teaspoon vanilla extract

COFFEE CAKE GLAZE

Whisk together powdered sugar, milk, butter, and vanilla until smooth. Drizzle over the cake while warm.

Hummingbird Cakes
with Cream Cheese Frosting

Yield: 1 (8-inch)3-layer cake or 6 (4-inch) 2-layer cakes

3 cups all-purpose flour

2 cups sugar

1 teaspoon baking soda

2 teaspoons ground cinnamon

$^1/_2$ teaspoon salt

3 eggs, lightly beaten

1 cup vegetable oil

$1^1/_2$ cups mashed ripe bananas

1 (8-ounce) can crushed pineapple with juice

$1^1/_2$ cups chopped pecans, divided

2 teaspoons vanilla extract

Hummingbird cake is a banana-pineapple spice cake that first appeared in Southern Living *magazine in 1978. My version of this classic Southern cake can be made as a large cake or as miniature individual cakes, perfect for making each dinner party guest feel special.*

Preheat oven to 350 degrees F. Prepare 3 (8-inch) round baking pans or 12 (4-inch) round baking pans with nonstick cooking spray or line with parchment paper.

In a large mixing bowl, stir together flour, sugar, baking soda, cinnamon, and salt. Add eggs and oil and stir just until combined, being sure not to overbeat the batter. Stir in bananas, pineapple, 1 cup pecans, and vanilla. Evenly divide batter between cake pans. If using 8-inch baking pans, bake for 30–35 minutes or until a toothpick inserted comes out clean. For 4-inch baking pans, bake for 24–26 minutes or until toothpick inserted comes out clean. Allow to cool for 10 minutes before turning out onto wire racks to cool completely.

CREAM CHEESE FROSTING

8 ounces cream cheese

$^1/_2$ cup unsalted butter

$3^1/_2$ cups powdered sugar

1 teaspoon vanilla extract

CREAM CHEESE FROSTING

Beat together cream cheese and butter until light and fluffy using a stand mixer. Add powdered sugar, 1 cup at a time, scraping down sides between each addition. Add vanilla and beat for 2–3 minutes. Frost cooled cakes and top with remaining pecans from cake ingredients.

Texas Sheet Cake

Yield: 14–16 servings

1 cup butter

1 cup water

1/2 cup unsweetened cocoa powder

1 cup light brown sugar

2 teaspoons vanilla extract

2 cups all-purpose flour

1 cup sugar

1/2 teaspoon salt

1 teaspoon baking soda

1/2 cup sour cream

2 large eggs, beaten

Born in Dallas, Texas, my love for Texas sheet cake began at a very young age. There is nothing better than a slice of this chocolate cake with its fudgy frosting and a big glass of ice cold milk. My daughter agrees—everything is bigger and better in Texas, after all.

Preheat oven to 350 degrees F. Spray a jelly roll pan or half-sheet (13 x 18-inch) pan with nonstick cooking spray or line with parchment paper.

In a large saucepan, combine butter, water, and cocoa powder over medium-high heat. Bring to a boil and remove from heat. Stir in brown sugar and vanilla. In a separate mixing bowl, combine flour, sugar, salt, and baking soda. Add flour mixture to saucepan and stir to combine. Add in sour cream and eggs, stirring until well combined and no lumps remain. Pour batter into the prepared pan, spreading evenly to sides and corners. Bake 15–20 minutes or until set. Allow to cool.

CHOCOLATE GLAZE

1/2 cup butter

1/4 cup unsweetened cocoa powder

1/3 cup milk

1 teaspoon vanilla extract

3 1/2 cups powdered sugar

1 cup pecans, coarsely chopped

CHOCOLATE GLAZE

Add butter, cocoa powder, and milk to a saucepan. Bring mixture to a boil. Remove from heat and stir in vanilla. Next, whisk in powdered sugar until smooth. Working quickly, spread glaze over cake using a rubber spatula. Top with pecans. Allow to set and cut into squares.

Pies &
Cobblers

*My three favorite Southern food
groups are pie, pie, and cobbler!*

Perfect Pie Crust

Yield: 8-10 inch pie crust

SINGLE CRUST

1/2 cup unsalted butter, chilled

1 1/4 cups all-purpose flour

1/4 teaspoon salt

1/4 cup ice water

DOUBLE CRUST

1 cup unsalted butter, chilled

2 1/2 cups all-purpose flour

1/2 teaspoon salt

1/2 cup ice water

FOOD PROCESSOR METHOD

Cut butter into 1/4-inch cubes and keep cold while prepping. In a food processor fitted with a steel blade, pulse together cold butter cubes, all-purpose flour, and salt. Once pulsed, the butter pieces should be pea size. Feed the water, a little bit at a time, through the feed tube of the processor while pulsing. Continue pulsing until the dough begins to form a ball, pulling away from the sides. Quickly remove dough and wrap in plastic wrap. Refrigerate for at least 1 hour. When ready to use dough, roll out on a lightly floured surface from center to edge. Turn and lightly flour dough so it does not stick to your surface. If dough splits on edges, simply pinch back together. Roll dough out until 3–4 inches larger than your pie pan. Carefully transfer to pie pan and press sides down gently, trimming edges as needed.

HAND METHOD

Combine flour and salt in a mixing bowl. Cut in the cubed butter. Using a pastry blender or by hand, work the butter into the flour until the texture resembles bread crumbs. Work quickly so the butter stays cold. Drizzle the water over the flour mixture and toss together to moisten the dough. Flip the dough out onto a counter surface and knead the dough together just until a ball forms. Quickly remove dough and wrap in plastic wrap. Refrigerate for at least 1 hour. When ready to use dough, roll out on a lightly floured surface from center to edge. Turn and lightly flour dough so it does not stick to your surface. If dough splits on edges, simply pinch back together. Roll dough out until 3–4 inches larger than your pie pan. Carefully transfer to pie pan and press sides down gently, trimming edges as needed.

TIP: *The less you handle your dough, the better. You don't want your hands to warm the dough. Pie crust can also be frozen at the dough stage for up to two months.*

Buttermilk Pie

Yield: 6–8 servings

1 recipe single-crust Perfect
Pie Crust (page 162) dough

$1/2$ cup butter, room
temperature

$1^1/2$ cups sugar

3 eggs, room temperature

3 tablespoons all-purpose
flour

2 teaspoons vanilla extract

1 tablespoon lemon juice

$1/2$ teaspoon nutmeg

1 cup buttermilk

This old-fashioned dessert is a sweet custard pie made with just a few ingredients. If you love crème brûlée, you must try this buttermilk pie.

Preheat oven to 350 degrees F. Roll out pie crust and fit into pie pan.

Using an electric mixer, cream together butter and sugar until light and fluffy. Add eggs, 1 at a time, mixing thoroughly after each addition. Reduce speed to low and add flour, vanilla, lemon juice, and nutmeg. Add the buttermilk and stir until blended. Pour batter into prepared pie crust. Cover the edges of pie crust with strips of aluminum foil to keep the crust from browning too much. Bake for 45–50 minutes. Allow pie to cool and refrigerate until ready to serve.

Brown Sugar Pie

Yield: 6–8 servings

1 recipe double-crust Perfect Pie Crust (page 162) dough, divided into 2 equal-size discs

1½ cups light brown sugar

¼ cup butter, melted and slightly cooled

3 eggs, divided

1½ teaspoons vanilla extract

Every family has a secret recipe. Brown Sugar Pie is ours. Well, it was a secret until I shared it (with family permission, don't you worry) in Pizzazzerie and it became the most popular recipe to date. It's our favorite pie for Thanksgiving and Christmas. We usually double the recipe to make two pies. Once I introduced my in-laws to Brown Sugar Pie, I learned to never arrive at their house over the holidays without at least one in hand.

Preheat the oven to 350 degrees F. Roll out 1 pie crust disc and fit into pie pan.

Combine sugar and butter in a mixing bowl and stir well. Lightly beat 2 eggs in a small bowl and whisk the eggs into the sugar and butter until just combined. Stir in vanilla, do not overwhisk. Pour into prepared pie pan.

Roll out remaining pie crust disc to cut in strips and braid. Add the decorative braided edges around the pie. Lightly beat remaining egg in a small bowl with 2 tablespoons water. Brush edge of pie crust with egg wash. Bake for 50–55 minutes. If pie crust begins to brown too much while baking, carefully cover edges of pie crust with aluminum foil. Allow to cool then refrigerate for at least 2 hours to set. Serve with a scoop of vanilla ice cream. **NOTE:** You can also make this pie without the decorative edge. You will only need 1 unbaked pie crust in this case.

TIP: *Sprinkle simple pies with edible floral petals for a whimsical touch.*

Peach Lattice Cobbler

Yield: 6–8 servings

1 recipe double-crust
Perfect Pie Crust (page 162)
dough, divided into 2 equal-
size discs

5 cups ripe peeled and
sliced peaches

1 tablespoon lemon juice

$1/2$ cup sugar

$1/2$ cup light brown sugar

1 teaspoon ground
cinnamon

$1/2$ teaspoon ground ginger

2 tablespoons cornstarch

3 tablespoons unsalted
butter

1 egg, lightly beaten

My maternal grandfather, Papa Horton, loved his sweets. Cobblers were at the top of his list. This is the dessert you serve someone right before you ask them for a favor.

Preheat oven to 450 degrees F. Roll out 1 pie crust disc and fit into pan, extending edge beyond the rim of pan. Refrigerate until ready to fill.

In a large bowl, sprinkle peaches with lemon juice. In a separate bowl, stir together sugar, brown sugar, cinnamon, ginger, and cornstarch. Pour sugar mixture over peaches, stir together gently, and spread onto pie crust. Slice butter in cubes and dot butter on top of peaches.

On a lightly floured surface, roll out second pie crust disc. Cut dough into $1/2$-inch strips using either a straight or fluted edge. Lay out strips on pie filling, creating a lattice pattern. You can also top pie filling with a full pie crust cut with slits.

In a small bowl, whisk together lightly beaten egg with 2 tablespoons water. Brush pie crust top with egg wash. Place pie pan on a baking sheet. Bake for 15 minutes then reduce the heat to 350 degrees F and bake for an additional 30–35 minutes or until crust is lightly golden. If the crust begins to brown too quickly, create a loose tent with aluminum foil to lay gently over the pie while baking. Remove from oven and allow to cool before serving.

Mini Pecan Pies

Yield: 30 mini pies

1 recipe double-crust
Perfect Pie Crust (page 162)
dough

$^1/_2$ cup packed dark brown
sugar

$^1/_4$ cup unsalted butter,
melted

$^1/_3$ cup light corn syrup

2 eggs, room temperature,
lightly beaten

$^1/_2$ teaspoon vanilla extract

$^1/_2$ teaspoon salt

2 cups finely chopped
pecans

30 pecan halves

I've hosted many a "pie party" over the years and these bite-size pop-in-your-mouth pecan pies are one of my very favorite recipes. Turn any of your own favorite pie recipes into "minis" for a sweet delight that won't have your guests fumbling with forks.

Preheat oven to 350 degrees F. Prepare 2 mini muffin tins with nonstick cooking spray. Roll out pie crust, and using a 2-inch round cookie cutter or fluted round ravioli cutter, cut out 30 mini pie rounds. Press them gently into prepared mini muffin tins. Keep tins refrigerated until ready to fill.

In a mixing bowl, whisk together brown sugar, butter, corn syrup, eggs, vanilla, and salt. Stir in chopped pecans. Fill each pie crust with pecan pie filling (about 1 to 2 teaspoons) and top with a pecan half. Bake 20–22 minutes or until filling is set and pie crusts are lightly golden. Allow to cool for 5 minutes before gently removing from pan.

Lemon Chess Pie

Yield: 6–8 servings

1 recipe single-crust Perfect Pie Crust (page 162) dough

1⅓ cup sugar

2 tablespoons all-purpose flour

⅛ teaspoon salt

3 eggs, room temperature

3 tablespoons butter, melted

1 tablespoon lemon zest

¼ cup fresh-squeezed lemon juice (about 2 lemons)

¼ cup powdered sugar

When life gives us lemons, we typically stick 'em in our sweet tea. If we're lucky enough to have extra, lemons send this quintessentially Southern chess pie over the top!

Preheat oven to 325 degrees F. Roll out pie crust and fit into pie pan.

In the bowl of an electric. mixer, stir together sugar, flour, and salt. Turn mixer on low and add in eggs, 1 at a time, incorporating well after each addition. Increase mixer speed to medium until mixture is pale yellow and frothy. Next, add in butter, lemon zest, and lemon juice. Beat until well blended. Pour pie mixture into prepared pie crust. Bake for 45 minutes. Remove from oven and allow to cool to room temperature. Refrigerate until ready to serve. Dust with powdered sugar just before serving.

TIP: *Microwave lemons (or limes) for 30 seconds to get more juice.*

Strawberry Pie

Yield: 8 (4-inch) mini pies

1 recipe double-crust
Perfect Pie Crust (page 162)
dough, divided into 2 equal-
size discs

6 cups hulled and sliced
fresh strawberries

1¾ cups sugar

4 tablespoons cornstarch

1 tablespoon (1 envelope)
unflavored gelatin

1½ teaspoons lemon juice

⅔ cup water

Whipped cream, for garnish

Down South, strawberry pie counts as a serving of fruit. Each May, our family eats strawberries all different ways, but this strawberry pie is our favorite.

Preheat oven to 450 degrees F. On a lightly floured surface, cut pie crusts and use a large cookie cutter to cut out 4-inch pie circles. Each pie crust should yield approximately 4 circles. Place pie dough circles in miniature pie pans (pies shown baked in 4½–inch pie pans). After placing the pie crusts into the pans, prick the bottoms of the crust with a fork and bake for 8–10 minutes. Allow crusts to cool completely.

In a mixing bowl, crush 2 cups strawberries using a potato masher or back of a large spoon. Combine the sugar, cornstarch, gelatin, lemon juice, and water in a saucepan. Stir in the mashed strawberries and mix well. Bring this mixture to a boil over medium heat, stirring constantly. Continue to cook and stir for 2 – 3 minutes. Remove from the heat and pour into a large bowl. Chill for 30 minutes in the refrigerator. Fold the remaining strawberries into the chilled mixture. Fill each pie crust with the strawberry filling and chill for several hours. Serve with a dollop of whipped cream. **NOTE:** To make one large deep dish strawberry pie instead of miniature pies, use 1½ recipes of the single-crust pie crust to make a deep dish pie and follow the instructions accordingly.

TIP: *Make small or miniature versions of your favorite pies for picnics and on-the-go entertaining. They're easier to eat and your guests will have room to try more than one flavor.*

Sweet Potato Pie

Yields: 6–8 servings

1 recipe single-crust Perfect Pie Crust (page 162) dough

1½ cups cooked, mashed sweet potatoes

½ cup firmly packed light brown sugar

1 (3.4-ounce) box vanilla pudding mix

½ cup evaporated milk

2 eggs, room temperature, beaten

4 tablespoons butter, softened

1 teaspoon pumpkin pie spice

1½ teaspoons vanilla extract

Move over pumpkin pie—this Southern stunner takes the blue ribbon at Thanksgiving. Add a dollop of whipped cream and you'll be in high heaven.

Preheat oven to 450 degrees F. Roll out pie crust and fit into pie pan.

Combine sweet potatoes, sugar, pudding mix, evaporated milk, eggs, butter, pumpkin pie spice, and vanilla in bowl of an electric mixer. Beat at medium speed until well blended. Pour mixture into pie crust. To prevent overbrowning, cover edge of pie with aluminum foil. Bake for 10 minutes and reduce temperature to 375 degrees F. Continue baking for another 40 minutes or until a knife inserted in the center comes out clean. Cool before serving and keep refrigerated.

PECAN TOPPING

1 cup chopped pecans

¼ cup light brown sugar

2 tablespoons maple syrup

¼ teaspoon salt

PECAN TOPPING

To make topping, mix all the ingredients in a sauce pan and heat until it comes to a boil. Remove from heat and allow to cool slightly. Spread over pie and serve.

Oven "Fried" Apple Hand Pies

Yield: 24 hand pies

6 recipes single-crust Perfect Pie Crust (page 162) dough

3 large apples, peeled and finely chopped

$1/2$ cup light brown sugar

$1/2$ teaspoon cornstarch

2 teaspoon ground cinnamon

$1/2$ teaspoon ground nutmeg

1 teaspoon lemon juice

1 teaspoon vanilla extract

1 egg, lightly beaten

2 tablespoons water

3 tablespoons butter, cubed into small pieces

Coarse sugar for sprinkling on top

These delectable folded apple pies are full of flavor and easy to eat. Serve them on a wooden board or platter at your next gathering.

Preheat oven to 400 degrees F. Line a large baking sheet with parchment paper.

On a lightly floured surface, roll out pie crusts to $1/4$-inch thickness. Cut 5-inch circles from the pie crusts. Each pie crust should yield around 4 circles.

In a large skillet, combine apples, brown sugar, cornstarch, cinnamon, and nutmeg and stir to combine. Cook and stir for 7–8 minutes or until apples begin to caramelize. Remove from heat and stir in lemon juice and vanilla extract.

Scoop 1 to 2 tablespoons of apple filling on 1 half of each pie circle. In a small bowl, whisk together the egg and water. Brush edges of pie circle with egg wash and fold pie over filling. Press the edges with a fork to seal. Brush remaining egg wash over pies. Use a sharp knife to cut small slits into the top of the pies. Sprinkle with coarse sugar. Place pies on prepared baking sheet and bake for 20–22 minutes or until golden brown. Allow hand pies to cool and serve.

TIP: *Serve any of your favorite fruit pies in a hand pie shape. They're perfect for taking to a tailgate or picnic.*

Carolina Blackberry Cobbler

Yield: 6–8 servings

BLACKBERRY FILLING

6 cups fresh blackberries

¼ cup brown sugar

¼ cup sugar

2 tablespoons cornstarch

Blackberries grow wild in upstate South Carolina, where my grandparents lived. I still remember carrying buckets of blackberries back to the house with scratched-up arms and legs. It was all worth it when my grandfather turned them into this blackberry cobbler, and it's still a dessert we enjoy every summer. The scoop of vanilla ice cream on top is a must!

BLACKBERRY FILLING

Preheat oven to 350 degrees F. Prepare a 9 x 13-inch baking dish with nonstick cooking spray.

Wash the blackberries and drain. In a large mixing bowl, toss the blackberries with sugars and cornstarch to coat evenly. Spread berries in baking dish.

COBBLER TOPPING

2 cups all-purpose flour

1½ cups plus 2 tablespoons sugar, divided

1 tablespoon baking powder

½ teaspoon salt

½ teaspoon cinnamon

½ teaspoon ground ginger

1 tablespoon vanilla extract

½ cup butter, melted

¾ cup milk

COBBLER TOPPING

In a mixing bowl, stir together flour, 1½ cups sugar, baking powder, salt, cinnamon, and ginger. Stir in vanilla, butter, and milk until combined—it will be slightly lumpy.

Spoon the batter over top of the blackberries and sprinkle with remaining of sugar (turbinado or sanding sugar works well too). Bake 50–55 minutes or until golden brown. Serve warm with a scoop of ice cream.

Cocktails
& Drinks

*The South's strong cocktail culture
means we don't just have one happy
hour. We begin with Bloody Marys in
the morning, enjoy Shoo-Fly Punch
on the porch in the afternoon, and sip
Tennessee whiskey while watching lightnin'
bugs and football as the sun sets.*

Brunchtime Bloody Mary

Yield: 6–8 servings

5 cups tomato juice

3 tablespoons lemon juice

3 tablespoons lime juice, divided

1 cup beef broth or beef bouillon

2 tablespoons Worcestershire sauce

1/2 teaspoon Tabasco sauce

1/2 teaspoon garlic powder

1/2 teaspoon prepared horseradish

1/4 cup Old Bay Seasoning

2 tablespoons sea salt

1 cup vodka

GARNISHES

Celery stalks, jalapeños (pickled and fresh), pickles, banana peppers, bacon, boiled shrimp, cherry tomatoes, olives, lemon slices, lime slices

The South can't claim fame to their origin, but Bloody Marys sure have become synonymous with everything from SEC brunch tailgates to piazza "porch" parties in the lowcountry. Garnish your Bloody Mary with a boiled shrimp and a slice of bacon for one of the South's finest cocktails.

In a blender, combine tomato juice, lemon juice, 2 tablespoons lime juice, beef broth, Worcestershire sauce, Tabasco sauce, garlic powder, and horseradish. Blend until smooth. Pour into a pitcher and refrigerate until chilled.

In a shallow plate, combine Old Bay Seasoning and sea salt. Pour remaining lime juice into a separate shallow plate. Dip each glass rim into lime juice and then into seasoning salt to rim. Fill each glass with ice and 1 ounce vodka. Next, pour the Bloody Mary mix on top until glass is full, and garnish.

TIP: *Set out all garnishes in pretty bowls and dishes. Let your guests garnish their own perfect Bloody Mary.*

Sparkling Apple Cider Sangria

Yield: 6 servings

1 (750-milliliter) bottle Champagne or prosecco

2½ cups apple cider

1 cup club soda

½ cup Disaronno (amaretto liqueur)

2 apples, sliced

Cinnamon sticks, for garnish

Every year, when the leaves begin to fall, I find a reason to celebrate just so I can serve this Sparkling Apple Cider Sangria. It has become our signature cocktail for the holiday season.

In a large pitcher, combine the Champagne, apple cider, club soda, and Disaronno. Stir until mixed and add in sliced apples. Pour and garnish with a cinnamon stick.

TIP: *When styling your party table, coordinate your florals and table decor to blend with your party menu. Orange, red, and deep pinks always make a beautiful autumn tablescape.*

Southern Sweet Tea

Yield: 8–10 servings

SIMPLE SYRUP

1 cup sugar

1 cup water

In the South, a front porch without a swing is like tea without sugar—incomplete. In the movie Steel Magnolias, *Dolly Parton declared that sweet tea was "the house wine of the South." Serve up this sweet iced tea all year round; it's a must for every occasion.*

SIMPLE SYRUP

In a small saucepan, heat sugar and water to boil and stir until sugar dissolves and forms the simple syrup. Remove from heat, allow to cool, pour into a container, and store in refrigerator.

SWEET TEA

2 quarts water, divided

8 regular-size black tea bags

⅛ teaspoon baking soda

1 cup Simple Syrup

Lemon slices and mint, for garnish

SWEET TEA

In a large saucepan, bring 1 quart (4 cups) of water to a boil. Once boiling, remove from heat and add tea bags (tie strings together for easy removal later) and baking soda. Allow to steep for 8–10 minutes. Remove tea bags. Stir in simple syrup. Pour into a large pitcher, add remaining water. **NOTE:** You can add additional water to taste. Serve sweet tea over ice, garnished with lemon slices and mint.

TIP: *Create your own sweet tea flavor varieties by infusing with fresh fruit slices, such as peaches, pineapple, or strawberries.*

Old-Fashioned Homemade Lemonade

Yield: 6 servings

2 cups sugar

5 cups water, divided

1½ cups fresh lemon juice

Lemon slices, for garnish

Every summer, my brother and I set up a lemonade stand outside our Meeting Street home in downtown Charleston. While the horse-carriage tour guides were busy telling the tales of General P. G. T. Beauregard, we were racking up a gold mine as the tourists lined up in front of our card table. Our mother had to keep rushing lemonade out to keep up with the crowds. We even made the cover of the Charleston Post and Courier *as up-and-coming entrepreneurs. Here's our famous lemonade recipe.*

Begin by making a simple syrup: in a large saucepan, heat sugar and 2 cups water to boil and stir until sugar dissolves into a syrup. Remove from heat and allow to cool to room temperature. In a large pitcher, add lemon juice, simple syrup, and remaining water. Add more water to taste. Serve with ice, and garnish with lemon slices.

TIP: *Float floral blooms in your lemonade (or other drinks) for a charming touch.*

Orange Mimosa Floats

Yield: 4–6 servings

1 pint orange sherbet

1 (750-milliliter) bottle Champagne or prosecco

A twist on the classic mimosa, orange sherbet is topped with Champagne for a party-perfect treat. Switch it up with your favorite sherbet flavors.

Fill each glass with a couple small scoops of orange sherbet. Top with champagne and serve!

TIP: *Head outside and use fresh garden clippings, such as ivy or nandina, for a charming touch to simple platters and trays.*

Brandy Alexander Milkshakes

Yield: 4 servings

1 quart vanilla ice cream

1/2 cup brandy

1/4 cup Cointreau (orange-flavored liqueur)

1/4 cup crème de cacao

1 teaspoon nutmeg

My parents used to order Brandy Alexander Milkshakes at a local Dallas bar after attending the symphony. My mother loved them so much that she went on a quest to recreate the recipe at home. They've since become a favorite, especially on Christmas Eve.

In a blender, combine ice cream, brandy, Cointreau, and crème de cacao. Mix well. Mixture will be thick. Pour into chilled glasses and top with freshly grated nutmeg just before serving.

Grapefruit Shoo-Fly Punch

Yield: 6–8 servings

½ cup sugar

½ cup water

2½ cups bourbon

1 cup ginger liqueur (such as Domaine de Canton)

2 cups grapefruit juice

2 teaspoons bitters

Grapefruit slices, for garnish

If there's one thing Southerners often say, it's "shoo fly." We gave this summertime bourbon punch a grapefruit twist and garnished it with fresh mint from the backyard.

Begin by making a simple syrup. Add sugar and water to a saucepan and bring to a boil, whisking to dissolve sugar. Allow simple syrup to cool.

Combine bourbon, ginger liqueur, grapefruit juice, bitters, and simple syrup, stirring well. Fill glasses with ice and top with punch. Garnish with fresh grapefruit slices. **NOTE:** If you like a sweeter drink, add more simple syrup.

Watermelon Mint Juleps

Yield: 6–8 mint juleps

MINT SIMPLE SYRUP

1 cup sugar

1 cup water

12 mint leaves

There's no better way to celebrate the Derby than with a frosty mint julep cup in hand. Watermelon Mint Juleps give this classic cocktail a fruity, sweet taste.

MINT SIMPLE SYRUP

Combine sugar and water in a small saucepan and bring to a boil, whisking to dissolve sugar. Remove from heat and add mint leaves. Allow to cool completely and refrigerate for 24 hours. Strain to remove mint.

JULEPS

4 cups cubed fresh watermelon

1¼ cups Mint Simple Syrup

3 cups bourbon

Crushed ice

Watermelon wedges or balls, for garnish

Mint leaves, for garnish

JULEPS

Purée watermelon in a blender or food processor and pulse until smooth. Use a sieve to remove pulp and seeds, leaving about 2 cups fresh watermelon juice. In a pitcher, combine Mint Simple Syrup, bourbon, and watermelon juice. Stir to combine. Fill mint julep glasses with crushed ice and top with watermelon mixture. Garnish with fresh watermelon and mint.

Holiday Spiced Punch

Yield: 25–30 servings

1 gallon apple cider

1 cup lemon juice

2 cups dark rum (optional)

1/2 cup cinnamon Schnapps (optional)

12 cinnamon sticks

4 teaspoons ground nutmeg

4 teaspoons whole cloves

The quintessential holiday beverage, this spiced punch will make your home smell like Christmas. We serve the kid-friendly version of this punch to my daughter and her friends every holiday, and they feel "oh so fancy" sipping this delightful drink.

Combine apple cider and lemon juice in a large pot. Add in rum and Schnapps, if using. Place the cinnamon sticks, nutmeg, and cloves in a 9-inch square of cheesecloth. Gather the cloth at the top and tie securely with a cotton string. Place the spice bag in the cider and simmer for 15–20 minutes over medium heat. This holiday spiced punch can be served hot or cold.

TIP: *Serve this punch with cinnamon stick stirrers.*

Perfect Party Punch

Yield: 35 servings

1 quart pineapple juice, chilled

1 quart orange juice, chilled

1 quart apple juice, chilled

2 quarts ginger ale or 1 (750-milliliter) bottle of Champagne, chilled

Bursting with fruit flavors, you'll find your party guests gathering around the punchbowl for seconds of this perfect party punch.

In a large punch bowl, combine pineapple, orange, and apple juices. Just before serving, pour in ginger ale or Champagne and stir until blended. Garnish with fresh fruit slices and flowers.

TIP: *Keep your punch ice cold throughout your party by making an ice ring. Freeze fruit juices in a bundt pan for at least 4 hours or until set. Dip the bottom of the pan into warm water for a few seconds and slide the ice ring out and into your punch bowl.*

Special Thanks

Thank you to my talented photographer, Kyle Dreier, for bringing our vision to life. I am forever grateful. We've been creating books together for more than years, and your mentorship and constant inspiration has meant the world to me.

Special thanks to my mother for your countless hours and talent. This book would not have been possible without you. There's no one I'd rather work beside.

To my editor, Katie Killebrew, for allowing me to pour my heart into this book and your patience in listening to my passionate enthusiasm for every detail of these pages. To everyone at Gibbs Smith for your hard work in making this book a reality.

Special thanks to Jared Olson for working your magic to set the scene, all while entertaining children and puppies with ease. Thanks to Victoria Clemmons, for your help and coordination behind the scenes.

To Chris, I could not have completed this book without you. Thank you for your hours of assistance, taste testing, set up, clean up, and everything in between, especially on the longest days. I love you.

Blakely, thank you for always bringing a smile to my face, even on the hardest days. My greatest joy in life is being your mother.

Special thanks Heidi, for your friendship and gracious assistance on set.

To Kate Beebe and Frontgate, for your gorgeous additions to these pages.

Thank you to Nancy Brown for your constant support of our endeavors.

To my father, for your never-ending encouragement and love.

To my brother, David, for your recipe assistance and listening ear.

Last but not least, a special thank you to the readers and followers of *Pizzazzerie*, you are the reason I can call this dream a career. I am forever grateful for your love and support.

Index

Growing up in the South, **Courtney Dial Whitmore** has always loved the art of presenting classic Southern foods with a modern twist and setting a tablescape with lots of pizzazz. In 2010, she launched her lifestyle site Pizzazzerie.com. Her work has been featured in *Southern Living*, *HGTV*, *Better Homes & Gardens*, and *Martha Stewart*. She is the author of four other books: *Pizzazzerie: Entertain in Style*, *Frostings, Candy Making For Kids, and Push-Up Pops*. She lives in Nashville with her husband and daughter.

Phronsie Dial is a creative stylist and tablescape designer who works on brand partnerships for Pizzazzerie.com. Over the past four decades, she has created countless DIY party ideas and crafts for magazines and news outlets. She also happens to be one-half of this mother/daughter duo as Courtney's mom.

Metric Conversion Chart

VOLUME MEASUREMENTS		WEIGHT MEASUREMENTS		TEMPERATURE CONVERSION	
U.S.	**METRIC**	**U.S.**	**METRIC**	**FAHRENHEIT**	**CELSIUS**
1 teaspoon	5 ml	1/2 ounce	15 g	250	120
1 tablespoon	15 ml	1 ounce	30 g	300	150
1/4 cup	60 ml	3 ounces	90 g	325	160
1/3 cup	75 ml	4 ounces	115 g	350	180
1/2 cup	125 ml	8 ounces	225 g	375	190
2/3 cup	150 ml	12 ounces	350 g	400	200
3/4 cup	175 ml	1 pound	450 g	425	220
1 cup	250 ml	2 1/4 pounds	1 kg	450	230